Claudi

Italy's Hidden Corners

Translation by
Rachel Stone and *Gokce Hazal Karabas*

historica

historica publishing
travel books

Italy's Hidden Corners

Original title: *I bei luoghi dell'Italia nascosta*

© 2018 Historica Publishing

Editorial direction
Francesco Giubilei

Series direction
Francesca Mazzucato

ROME
ISBN 978-88-33370-29-3
1st edition – october 2018

I want to take you on a journey that excites us as we walk side by side.

In today's fast-paced society, everything is taken for granted. We look without seeing, we hear without listening, we taste without savouring.

A falling leaf can become an animated painting as it slowly swirls and conveys its sensuality, unabashed as it gracefully reaches the silky bed where millions of leaves have danced with elegance. And yet, some will only see a falling leaf.

The creak of a closing gate becomes enchanted as it opens the doors to your imagination, opening your heart to a magical world of lords and ladies. And yet, others hear nothing more than the sound of an iron-rusted gate.

When cooked with patience, the bitter chicory and acrid onions blend to create an aroma of love. And yet, there are those who will taste nothing more than a simple soup.

It is all a matter of emotion, of feeling and touching with the eyes, mind, and heart.

Hand in hand, the path becomes evermore beautiful as we slowly begin this journey together. One foot behind the other, and never looking back, much like life.

Known in Neapolitan dialect as "Lo cunto de li cunti", or "Tale of Tales", this collection of 17th century fairy tales by Giambattista Basile was the inspiration for Matteo Garrone's film. The setting of the film is provided by the mystical green forests and gardens, historical castles, ancient palaces, and small towns of central and southern Italy, and provides a very real background to the famous director's fantasy-drama film.

Garrone once said: "It is highly likely that you will leave the movie theatre after seeing "Tale of Tales" with a curiosity and desire to know where the incredibly beautiful scenes were shot. Some may recognize a few of the places, but most will not".

Scene after scene, Matteo Garrone's film, "Tale of Tales", allows your mind to soar above beautiful landscapes that enrich the story and the scenography, and invites the question "Where could they have possibly filmed these scenes?" Maybe Indonesia, or perhaps New Zealand? While watching Garrone's film in the small, but intimate Cinema Eliseo in Cesena, I was overcome with a sudden feeling of déjà-vu. As I watched the scene of people running, and a beautiful, semi-naked young maiden with long hair, it hit me. I practically jumped out of my seat, declaring: "That's Sasseto!" My wife and my daughter looked at me like I was crazy, gesturing a clear signal for me to be quiet. My daughter alarmingly questioned if I had fallen asleep, and suggested that perhaps I had been dreaming. I quickly realized my enthusiasm had been a bit over the top for such a cosy movie theatre, so I continued my revelation in a whisper: "I know that place, I was practically born there!" If they thought I was losing my mind before, when I told them I was born there they officially had their proof. However, I had truly recognized the place where I used to play as a child, and a few scenes later, I was certain. It was the Bosco Monumentale of Sasseto: a magical place full of my most treasured childhood memories, and Torre Alfina, a small hamlet located in the municipality of Acquapendente found in a very special part of central Italy. Anyone with the opportunity to visit this sliver of land, located in the northern part of the region of Lazio, situated between the provinces of Terni, Siena, and the western part of Grosseto, would be remiss to do so without feeling as though they have found themselves in a distant fairy tale. Surrounded by enormous trees soaring toward the open skies, thick amounts of moss cover the white and grey boulders, visible every now and then amongst the endless green. Giant, grey, and oddly gathered as if ritualistically or defensively placed by ancient man, these huge stones are also known as "white boulders" because of their colour. Upon closer inspection, the trick is quickly revealed: the rocks are covered in lichens, algae and moss. When I used to play in the forest as a child, the most fascinating and meaningful aspects of this mystical forest were the giant ferns. The indelible memories are forever present, reinforced by the unforgettable aroma of the forest that brings back a sea of emotions. Shortly after seeing Garrone's movie, I was consumed by the desire to visit the forest again. Returning with my cousin Ombretta and her husband Roberto, who both know the secret pathways intimately, I felt as though I were diving back into my past. Today, the ferns seem less "gigantic", and yet, somehow, just as immense, and while I almost seem to recognize the trees, in turn they seem to recognize me as well. They give the appearance of a welcoming bow, while maintaining their enchanted nature, and take on a strange form as they strain themselves toward the rays of sunlight so essential to the natural process of photosynthesis. One by one they present themselves as puppets controlled by unseen strings that with every touch of wind seem to speak amongst themselves in a language forgotten by adults, yet remembered only by children. They hear and understand the conversations of these kind-hearted giants; they ask questions and immerse themselves in the tree hollows created by time and weathering. These beckoning figures capture our attention and show us the way. Ignoring the natural clues of the forest can prove troublesome and losing your way can quickly become an unfavourable reality. All the same, allowing yourself to be immersed in the rules of the game, letting your mind run free, paves the way for a new discovery with each step as tree trunks, flowers and ferns slowly morph into animals, faces, and other images familiar only within each of us. This land knows many truths, and has observed many carefree joys. It has borne witness to the fear, hunger and death of the Second World War, as well as provided essential refuge beneath piles of grey rock and hollowed caves large enough for small groups of people looking to flee the bombings.

Walking along the winding trails, you quickly understand that this place has also hosted an abundance of love stories, like those of a fairy tale. Everywhere you look, you find yourself surrounded by the allurement of Mother Nature, which brings peace to the body and soul, and leaves room for prosperous ideas of the future while simultaneously preserving fond memories of the past. And, with a glance toward the magnificent castle, which the Marquis Cahen recovered from a semi-abandoned state, we are reminded of the forest's own past. In honour of the love and appreciation for this special space, they preserved the forest and created the Garden of the Torre Alfina. Today, you can visit these gardens and imagine yourself walking alongside King Edward, who so cherished the forest that his final wish was to be buried there in a mausoleum constructed specifically for him.

The enchanting places carefully selected by Garrone and all easily reached, give way to more scenes, more places, and more déjà-vu. That being said, you now know the story that sparked the motivation for this book, which aims to summarize all the necessary information and instructions for visiting these "hidden corners" of Italy.

PART ONE

LAZIO

The small town of Torre Alfina is a subdivision of the city of Acquapendente situated along the northern border of Alfina's highlands, about 600 metres above sea level and about 90 km from the region's capital city.

The castle can be seen from kilometres around, making it impossible to get lost along the single road that leads to the castle and ends in the central square. From the square, a narrow street grants access to the watchtower and castle built in the High Middle Ages.

The Castle

The imperial neo-gothic style of the castle of Torre Alfina, clad in grey stones from nearby Bagnoregio, is inarguably one of the most fascinating establishments in the Umbria-Tuscan-Lazio regions. Having been changed over time from its original Medieval and Renaissance styles, two aspects remain from this 6th century structure: the internal courtyard and the first floor of one wing with a monumental stone-fireplace and decorative emblem celebrating various family dynasties.

The castle is a place where ancient traditions have been handed down over time, and mix with individual histories of the buildings constructed along the narrow alleys that seem to bow to the castle.

The palace, built near the tower, has had various proprietors throughout history. The first were the Risentii in the 13th century, followed by the Monaldeschi of Orvieto from the Cervara family who owned the palace from the late 1200s until the second half of the 1600s. This primitive castle owes its Renaissance style to Sforza Cervara. When Italy became a republic in 1946, the castle became part of the municipality of Acquapendente, as it remains today.

By the end of the 1800s, Count Edward Cahen, who later became the marquis of Torre Alfina, bought all stately properties. Edward had the entire Monaldeschi Palace restored but unfortunately died before seeing it completed. His final wish was to be buried in a gothic-style mausoleum-tomb in his beloved forest-garden of Sasseto that he had strived to make accessible via small pathways built among the rocks. Teofilo Rodolfo, Edward's son, would later complete this project and furnish the castle with studied elegance and carried out the construction of a large garden above the forest.

Today, Torre Alfina is a medieval village that appreciates and maintains its own history, culture, nature and folklore. Sasseto is listed among the official Forrestal Monuments of Italy, and the town itself was recently chosen to be part of a national archive of "Italy's Most Beautiful Towns".

The Monumental Forest of Sasseto

Amongst the trees, ferns, rocks, and moss of this enchanted town, Garrone chose to film some of his scenes from the tale of the "Due Vecchie", or "The Two Old Ladies" in the 60-hectare secular mesophyll forest, inhabited by more than 25 species of trees reaching heights of up to 25-30 metres with trunks over 1 meter in diameter. The rich flora and fauna that emerge from the rare elements found in this majestic forest make it a particularly unique place.

The forest is noted for its lavish vegetation, abundance of rock, and a notable lack of trees. The name Sasseto, meaning "large rock", is derived from the ancient volcanic system now covered by the lavish vegetation. However, much to the dismay of botanists, a small community of trees does exist in this area. Theoretically, the ecological conditions necessary for the types of trees found in these woods differ greatly from those found in the Sasseto forest. And yet, we find species such as beech, oak, maple, and elm, all sharing this vital space with tilia, holly, chestnuts, hornbeams, and holm oaks.

These trees, along with a display of undergrowth, a wide variety of flowers including orchids, and different varieties of ferns, demonstrate nature's ability to co-exist among ecologically different species. As curious onlookers, we are reminded of how much more vast this area could be without centuries of mankind's influence in simplifying and reducing forests to only a few types of trees. Because the forest is privately owned, ecological niches have remained intact, making it a complete forest populated by birds and different animals from wild boars that scurry away at the slightest sound, to the small dormouse that quickly runs up the trunks of the trees in search of a refuge where its small family will hibernate during the long, cold months of winter.

The Flower Museum

"An evoking journey through the story of flowers housed in a museum: understanding and learning to respect nature through a path of interactive games, stories and facts".

Before heading off to a tasty lunch in one of several delicious restaurants or agritourism spots of the surrounding areas, or to savour some creamy artisanal gelato from Sarchioni's Gelateria, one final spot is worth stopping for: the Flower Museum.

With over a thousand different species of plants and flowers growing in the territory, as well as a large variety of wildlife, it is easy to understand the motivation behind this naturalistic museum. The scope of the museum, housed in the Monte Rufeno Nature Reserve, is to bring to life the abundant treasures and traditions of the surrounding areas. Using interactive technology and multimedia tools, the museum offers an opportunity to learn about and discover the biodiversity and environmental history of the natural world.

Located in a refashioned country house, "Il Casale Giardino", about 2 km from the medieval town of Torre Alfina, the museum is situated in one of the most striking valleys of the area, with an extensive collection of rare species of animals, plants and flowers.

Natural mechanisms are celebrated through a compelling display of the diverse plant and animal life that lives within these woods, as well as the ecological importance of such habitats. As you enter this world of flowers and learn about the ecological changes that have taken place over time, with particular attention given to its relationship with the animal kingdom and mankind, you eventually arrive to the final room of the museum dedicated to the local celebration of Pugnaloni, which will be explained later. The history of the old "casale" itself is also part of the museum, and houses the "Tree of Life", implemented by the ethologist Giorgio Celli of the University of Bologna, and gives an insightful representation of the relationship between insects and flowers.

Careful attention is given to a variety of media such as pictures, models, computers, educational workshops and games, in an attempt to allow visitors to directly interact with the information on a personal level using all five senses.

In regards to the area beyond the museum, the "Sentiero Natura del Fiore" or the "Natural Path of Flowers", an outdoor path of average difficulty, guides visitors on a discovery of local plants and flowers complete with about twenty informative panels and educational bee hives in which visitors can observe bees interacting with their natural environment. In addition to the educative trail, a large botanical garden with a picnic area provides a nice place to relax amongst the beauties of the forest.

For more information:
L'Ape Regina Co-op organizes excursions and guided tours in collaboration with the Municipality of Acquapendente, Alfina Castle and site managers of the town. For reservations, contact L'Ape Regina Co-op. Tel: +39 0763-730065, or the Tourism Office of Acquapendente toll free: 800-411834 (press 0 for the extension number).

E-mail:
info@museodelfiore.it;
eventi@laperegina.it

Further information:
http://www.museodelfiore.it;
www.laperegina.it

The small town of Acquapendente is located in northern Lazio near San Casciano dei Bagni in the province of Siena (a well-known city surrounded by forests and hot springs), and is neighboured by other small towns to the west in the province of Grosseto near the Tyrrhenian Sea. To the east, in the province of Terni, in Umbria, symbols of a once lived past are evident in Castel Giorgio and Castel Viscardo. The small town of Allerona also sits to the east and shares part of the Monte Rufeno Nature Reserve with Acquapendente, which partly extends into Tuscany.

The pristine nature of the territory surrounding Acquapendente becomes immediately notable to anyone who chooses to visit, and represents the true wealth of the region. For this reason, specific policies were implemented to create jobs relating to the fields of environmental protection and eco-friendly tourism, which aim to make the most of the valuable natural resources and rich plant and animal life of the Monte Rufeno Nature Reserve. Acquapendente's origins date back to the Etruscan era, and the physical attributes of the locals still reflect the Etruscan characteristics. The Romans also inhabited this area until the Longobardi conquered it. Intersected by the Via Cassia, which connects Rome and Florence, Acquapendente is about 10 km from Lake Bolsena, another enchanting place untouched by man that offers a glimpse into the past.

The ancient name, *Acqua Pens*, gives us a clear understanding as to the origins of its current name, and is located near numerous small waterfalls that flow into the Paglia River, a tributary of the Tiber. The land of Acquapendente is home to an assortment of fountains, among which are the famous "Mascheroni" limestone fountains of glimmering water that continuously flows throughout all four seasons.

When taking a closer look at the location of Acquapendente, the way the town has developed begins to take on a new significance. The current urban centre seems as though it originated as a small hamlet with the focal point being the Santa Vittoria Church built between the 5th and 6th centuries. The city sits along the Via Francigena, a historically significant road that once led pilgrims to Rome. Today, this road has been rediscovered and given new significance due to its similarities with the pilgrimage route of Santiago of Compostela and its crucial connection between

Rome and central Europe, especially with France from which its name derives.

From every direction, the tower known as the Torre del Barbarossa, or Barbarossa Tower, extends a welcoming greeting anyone paying a visit to Acquapendente. Surrounded by pine trees, this place provides an ideal spot for people both young and old to escape the stresses of daily life. One of Acquapendente's most significant and historical events is the "Miracolo della Madonna del Fiore" or the "Miracle of Our Lady in Bloom" commemorating what took place during the battle between the Papal Reign and the Roman Empire which led to the rebellion, and consequential liberation of Acquapendente's citizens who were against Barbarossa's domination. Every year, on the third Sunday of May, Acquapendente commemorates this victory with the "Pugnaloni" celebration, whose name derives from the handmade mosaic panels composed of flower petals and leaves. Hundreds of young people from the surrounding area participate in this unique event dating back to one of the most important chapters of Acquapendente's history: the 1166 liberation from the tyranny of Frederick I, otherwise known as "Barbarossa". The legend tells of oppressed farmers who gathered under a dried up, old tree. As the king's requests grew more and more unbearable, the farmers decided to rebel. According to the most sceptical member of the group, all strategies were futile since the emperor had an entire army and weaponry, whereas they possessed mere agricultural tools. Almost as if to challenge the other farmers, the most sceptical of the group stated "We will defeat Barbarossa only when this poor cherry tree blooms again!" The next day, much to the astonishment of the townsmen, two farmers announced the tree had miraculously blossomed again. Taken as a sign of protection from the Virgin Mary, a revived sense of courage and strength united the citizens of Acquapendente, who rose in rebellion to defeat the emperor and take down his castle. From that day forward, they have celebrated this victory with a town-wide gathering in mid-May. These legends have been passed down from one generation to the next so as to never be forgotten. In fact, eight centuries later, the celebration of the Madonna del Fiore (The Lady in Bloom), also referred to as the Mezzomaggio (mid-May), continues to be deeply felt and honoured by the community with the Pugnaloni representing freedom from all forms of oppression. The ancestors of these Pugnaloni are known as Pungoli, ancient agricultural tools farmers used to decorate with flowers and use during the procession of a cherry wood statue of the Lady in Bloom, perhaps the very wood from the legend. Over the centuries, the Pugnaloni eventually replaced the pungoli. These handcrafted panels, typically 2.60 metres in width and 3.60 metres in height, are covered in flower petals and leaves, giving shape and colour to each and every nuance of the original design. While the technique used to create these works of art are similar to that of mosaics, only organic materials are used in order to give a natural effect to the panels. Experience passed down from one generation to the next has taught the artists how to pick only the most resistant and strong flower petals, which they then carefully glue on in order to preserve their freshness and colour. The various techniques used to secure the leaves and petals result in truly original and striking mosaics. The 15 Pugnaloni are all created by the youth of the area. This treasured contest spurs widespread research in which people scour the surrounding areas for as many types of flowers and leaves they can find. On the morning of the celebration, the Pugnaloni are displayed in the streets of the city's town centre, the main squares, and corners decorated for the celebration. At the end of the day, the Pugnaloni are then carried inside the Duomo, or cathedral, where they remain until the following year.

The Cathedral

When arriving to the small town of northern Lazio from Rome, a lovely, tree-lined road guides you toward the 10th century cathedral of Acquapendente. The natural landscape and small town surrounding this large building renders it even more grandiose and imposing. The history of this cathedral is considered part of the legend of Matilda of Westphalia, the mother of the emperor Otto I, who planned to travel from Germany to Rome to build a church dedicated to the Holy Sepulchre. However, upon reaching Acquapendente she was forced to stop for longer than she had foreseen due to the fact that the mules carrying the gold stubbornly stopped dead in their tracks and refused to budge an inch. In the peaceful little town, Matilda was able to sleep deeply, and began to have very vivid dreams. One night, she dreamt that the behaviour of the mules was the result of Divine Will, indicating that the destined city for the cathedral was not Rome, but Acquapendente. And so, Acquapendente was thereby named the new "chosen" city for the church.

This important historical moment led to Acquapendente becoming part of the patrimony of Saint Peter and was established as the episcopal seat of the Diocese of Orvieto. However, coexistence proved difficult due to the fact that Acquapendente wished to declare independence by capitalizing on its strategic location between the Marquisate of Tuscany and the Catholic Church (patrimony of Saint Peter), and therefore refused to be subordinate to Orvieto. This conflict eventually led to the first war between Orvieto and Acquapendente.

In 1649, the basilica was exalted to "Cathedral" in recognition of its role for pilgrims and cripples who would stop to pray in the church in hopes of miraculous cures. The cathedral is divided in three naves by pillars, with overhead apses and transepts. The 11th century Romanesque crypt located below the altar is of particular interest for its unusual arrangement of pillars, dividing the space into nine aisles. Referred to as "Il Duomo" by the people of Acquapendente, this cathedral contains a holy relic of its own: a blood-stained stone believed to come from Holy Sepulchre of Jerusalem that is preserved in the crypt. Built in the second half of the 11th century, the Romanesque style of the crypt is of special interest and great importance for Italy due to its ancient origins and particular architectural traits, including individual columns with capitolli (topmost member of the column) of which no two are alike, and form peculiar archways. The Cathedral is further enriched by two bas-reliefs, accredited to Agostino di Duccio: Tobias and the Angel and the Victory of Saint Michael over the Dragon.

The Church of Saint Francis

Dating back to a time prior to Saint Francis' birth, another religious building worth visiting is the Church of Saint Francis, whose name is derived from the Franciscan monks who have lived there since 1253. The adjacent three-story bell tower is from the Renaissance era (1506), however the gate dates back to the 11th century. Present in the façade is a beautiful rose window adorning the structure. Originally, the church had a more Gothic style, but was later adapted to a more Baroque style in 1747.

The Julia de Jacopo Tower

In the Medieval period, city walls surrounded Acquapendente. Much of the ancient, towering walls have since been destroyed, but a few remnants still remain, among which the Roman "porta" or door, also referred to as the Torre Julia de Jacopo in memory of a brave woman who managed to secure the door to the city when Acquapendente came under attack by Count Orsini's army in 1550. Recently remodelled and located near the cathedral, Julia de Jacopo Tower continues to be a beautiful part of the city and is used today as an information centre.

The Via Francigena

For centuries, this ancient road was an important resource for Acquapendente and anyone looking to take a spiritual journey. As a main route for pilgrims, it has always been considered a cultural point of interest and the perfect opportunity to meet people from different backgrounds. It was also considered an important commercial avenue due to the exchanging of goods from all over Europe.

The original route was different from what it is today. Historically, pilgrims began their journey from the Porta della Ripa and followed that which today is the Via Rugarella and reached the central square now named after the surgeon and anatomist Fabrizio Girolamo, a contemporary and friend of Galileo. The Via Francigena continued along today's Via XV Maggio, passing in front of the Church of Santa Vittoria, and eventually arriving at the Santo Sepolcro cathedral. From here, the pilgrims would exit from the Porta Romana, located near the Julia de' Jacopo Tower. Over the years, the layout has undergone various changes. Modern day pilgrims now primarily enter through the Porta Fiorentina, and from here continue on the Via Malintoppa, which connects with the Via Cesare Battisti and eventually Via Roma, and ends at the cathedral.

How to get there
Getting to Acquapendente by car is easy thanks to the Cassia state highway, about 130 km north of Rome and 90 km south of Siena. The closest interstate exit is Orvieto (A1).

Itinerary
You can easily visit Acquapendente on foot. Walking is the easiest way to take your time in each corner of the city and observe the beautiful buildings built in the 1500s, such as the Bishop's Palace and the Viscontini Palace where the influence of artists from Tuscany is well observed in the rustication of the adornments.

The Cassia state highway leads you out
of Acquapendente towards Rome. After a few
kilometres, you will find yourself at Lake Bolsena,
a crater lake with nearly 90 km of shoreline and
deep, crystal blue waters. Until just a few decades
ago, fishermen used to quench their thirst simply
by reaching their hand into the lake and taking a
drink.

However, runoffs from modern day farming
practices and residues from pesticides have slowly
polluted the lake rendering the water non-potable.
Nevertheless, Lake Bolsena is considered one of the
cleanest in Europe. The majestic sunsets highlight
the two small islands standing out against the
enchanting towns of Marta and Capodimonte that
charm locals and lure visitors.

The islands are accessible from three main
harbours: Capodimonte, Bolsena, and Marta.
Renting small boats from one of these three
locations, or taking one of the ferryboats that
travels to the islands daily make visits easy, and

the two islands are well worth a few hours of time and attention.

Continuing along our journey, you will soon arrive to the small town of Bolsena, the namesake of the lake. The town is famous for the legend of the Eucharist miracle of 1263, which occurred in the Basilica of Santa Cristina. The celebration of Santa Cristina is perfect for anyone who enjoys local festivities. On the evening of the 23rd and the morning of the 24th of July, the "mysteries" of Santa Cristina are represented in a series of lifelike plastic paintings that recall the events of the life and martyrdom of the young saint. Apart from the beautiful beach, other local attractions include the Monaldeschi Castle della Cervara, home to the Lake Bolsena Museum, as well as the archaeological site of Poggio Moscini.

This would be a good point in the trip to deviate slightly from the path, leaving Cassia behind and heading towards the "ghost town" of Civita di Bagnoregio, near the beautiful town of Orvieto. For those who have never been to this town, it is certainly worth a visit. Now home to only a few residents, its location renders it especially fascinating, and the emotions it is capable of evoking are almost impossible to describe in words. It is therefore necessary to simply schedule a time in the itinerary for this tuff-built town. Over the years, landslides have slowly eroded the hillside, isolating it from the city of Bagnoregio. Today, a long pedestrian bridge connects this hillside to the modern world, and on a foggy day the bridge becomes invisible to the untrained eye, giving the appearance of an island in the middle of nowhere. On these occasions, the beauty of the view of the valley is obviously a bit lost, however it also creates the idea of entering into a romantic and mysterious scene. Many Americans and Germans have fallen in love with this place, so much so that they have bought and restored a few buildings to make them inhabitable again.

Turning back toward Cassia, the dome of the Cathedral of Montefiascone peaks through the high trees, giving the slightest glimpse of the Renaissance building attributed to Michele Sanmicheli and completed during the second half of the 1600s by Carlo Fontana, the brain behind the design of the impressive dome and beautiful gateway.

Sitting triumphantly at 600 metres above sea level, Montefiascone permits its residents to rule over the vast landscape and glimmering lake over which the town prevails. In fact, this geographical positioning allows for perfect military defense and has been the centre of many wars of conquest.

Montefiascone is the most populated residential area in the northern province of Viterbo with widespread cultivation of wine grapes, home to the flourishing development of the esteemed wine "EST! EST! EST!"

The wine, however, is noted for more than

just its exceptional quality, it is where history and myth meet. The legend tells of Giovanni Defuck, a German Bishop of the court of Henry V and wine connoisseur, who sent his prelate to Montefiascone with the task of tasting the local wine. The wine scout was told to write "EST!" (Latin for "there is") on the door of the tavern if the wine was especially good. The messenger was so convinced by the deliciousness of the "Moscatello" tavern that he enthusiastically gave it the now famous "EST! EST! EST!"

Defuck enjoyed the wine so much that he stayed in Montefiascone until he drank himself to death in 1113, leaving his possessions to the town under one condition: each year, the townsmen must pour a bottle of his beloved wine over his grave.

As a historically and archeologically rich province, it is clear to see why this area has much to commemorate. On a sunny afternoon, you can easily enjoy Romanesque churches such as the S. Flavino church, constructed in the 13th century with a lower and upper church. Built in 1032 and comprised of an even older chapel built by the Lombardi craftsmen, the column capitals dividing the three naves show influence of the Etruscan order. At the back of the church, creating a large arch, three apses reflect the framework of Byzantine architecture.

The vaulted ceiling, with posterior Romanesque archways, and anterior Gothic archways, meets in the middle of the central nave, allowing an open view of the upper church. A large entryway and three arches accent the incomplete façade, built in 1262, with loggia balconies dating back to the 6th century. Housed within the church is the tomb of the aforementioned German nobleman Giovanni Defuck, the "discoverer" of the local "EST! EST! EST!" wine.

Another site that allows visitors to relish in breath-taking views is the Rocca dei Papi, a main attraction of the area. Its position at the peak of the hill allows for a dominating panorama over all of Tuscia, Viterbo, and Monti Comini.

Only a few kilometres from the Cassia state highway are the magnificent medieval walls of Viterbo, which allow access to the city through the ancient gates of Porta Fiorentina.

As one of the first cities to emerge on the peninsula in 1095, and the capital of Christianity during the Middle Ages, Viterbo was considered a very powerful city until it became part of the Papal States for nearly a millennium. In 1870 it became part of the Reign of Italy. The medieval neighbourhood is a treasure that slowly reveals its best-kept secrets hidden around every corner.

With every turn, beautiful and famous ochre-coloured buildings are sure to charm anyone who chances upon them. It was from the Piazza San Lorenzo where Orson Welles placed the sea beyond the arcades in Piazza delle Erbe, and where Fellini filmed "I Vitelloni" and the extraordinary Alberto Sordi played the role of policeman Otello Celletti atop a motorcycle in 1960. More recently, the streets and neighbourhoods of Viterbo, surrounded by impressive buildings, set the stage for the television series "Il Maresciallo Rocca" starring Stefania Sandrelli and Gigi Proietti.

The Pope's Palace

Upon arriving in the central piazza of San Lorenzo, the Palazzo dei Papi (Pope's Palace), strikingly appears all at once. As Viterbo's most important historical monument, Palazzo dei Papi is commonly known as the "Palazzo Papale". The original structure of the building sits much as it does today, originally the seat of the Bishop Curia, and eventually was enlarged, at the request of Pope Alexander IV, to allow sufficient residency for the popes when the seat of the Papal Curia was moved to Viterbo in 1257. A large audience hall was also added, known today as the "Aula (o Sala) del Conclave" because it housed the first and longest conclave in history from 1268-1271, which lasted 1,006 days. Taking time to pause and slowly absorb the surroundings of this impressive display is the only way to truly appreciate the Palazzo dei Papi. Even the drafts of air that blow through the massive arches seem as though they were deliberately put there to assist the visitor, as if to say, "Don't forget to breathe". At the end of the long staircase, you find yourself looking out on an ancient landscape.

A Stroll to Villa Lante

If you close your eyes for a moment, it is easy to imagine strolling along with a Viterbo local, happily listening to her accompanying words.

"With our backs to the medieval city of Viterbo, we leave behind a city full of rich history and traditions, with its double-arched windows, its impressive San Pellegrino neighbourhood and piazzas with majestic fountains that bring the pungent aromas and bustle of the ancient markets back to life. Today, we will take the long road that will slowly bring us to the sanctuary of the Madonna della Quercia. A staircase takes us up to the church, with the imposing bell-tower at its side. The simplicity of the architectonic lines fuse together with the grandiosity of the entire complex, leaving you in shock as it fills the eye and leaves just enough space for the imagination. We find ourselves in 1467. 'Do you see the horseman escaping his enemies?' He's right there, at the foot of the oak tree, where the painted tile of the illustrated Virgin Mary holding baby Jesus in her arms hangs. And here we have the miracle. The horseman becomes invisible and just like that, his life is saved.

Let's keep walking. Let's coast along the path, almost caressing the antique villas, and observing the majestic trees that gently lose their vibrant yellowed, tired leaves to the long autumn months, with a winter hesitant to arrive. Out there somewhere, the noise of traffic lingers, but with a bit of concentration you can find the silence deep within you. A few kilometres later it still accompanies you along the road that will open the doors to your soul.

Crossing the first bridge our gaze is lost amongst the wide valleys and calm, solemn gardens of the villa. As soon as we arrive to the second bridge, 'look to the left and you will see the tower of Bagnaia, to the right the monumental trees that hide the garden of wonders'. A few steps ahead, beyond the external square, we move along the road that brings us in front of a large gate, and a few seconds later we finally arrive at the Villa Lante. I secretly watch, waiting for your astonished expression. We go through the door, and see the fountain of Pegasus, the winged horse that with a stomp of its hoof makes water gush from the rocks, meanwhile, from above, the Three Graces and Muses blow water into the small lake and the four Nereids spray the water toward the sky. If we climb the stairs to the left, we will immediately go towards the 'giardino all'italiana,' however for now 'I want to take you to the park, between the century-old holly oaks, where my mother would take me as a child. If you pay close attention, perhaps you can still hear her calling to me because it is a hunting reserve, but today we can simply rest seeing as we are in 1556 and the cardinal Gian Francesco De Gambara commissioned the architect Jacopo Barozzi, also known as "il Vignola", to design a work of great value and beauty'. In fact, between the park and the garden a perfect harmony exists among the work of man and the work of nature, so much so that fountains and water games cheer up the soul and warm our hearts. 'Now, if you would like, let's climb the surrounding wall, and walk down to the entrance of the gardens'. A stream begins high on the cliff, quickly flows down, and crosses the villa. The water seems as though many fountains host it, as if to break its descent until it reaches the embrace of the Fontana dei Quattro Mori, divided in four basins each with a small boat in the centre used by a warrior.

'Do you see the two small palaces reaching out to welcome us?' The palaces have stuccoed coffered ceilings and impressive frescoes, however let's start with the grotto of the Diluvio (flood), that perfectly demonstrates the seamless harmony between man and nature, at least until Nature commands our undivided attention. The water scurries between the rocks, the vegetation and the caverns before tumbling into the fountain of the Dolphins. What a sight it is to see the marriage between the basin and the vases. It is the reign of Neptune that dominates the earth during a flood. As the water regains its strength, it emerges from the claws of a shrimp, and flows down toward the Fountain of Giants that symbolizes the Arno and the Tiber. 'Look at the two enormous statues that almost seem as if they were taking a nap'. Suddenly, the water grows calm and returns to its silent and peaceful nature at the table of the cardinal, a huge marble table, intersected by a brook to maintain the freshness of fruits and vegetables at mealtime. 'Don't you find it to be a genius idea?' And then, the water begins its tumultuous flow in the fountain of the

Lumini. 'You're right!' They look like the small flames of many silver candles as it goes down, down, down, to the Fountain of the Four Deaths with the four ebony statues commissioned by Cardinal Montalto.

'Such splendour, don't you think? Shall we walk the path from the other direction? Perfect, let's climb the stairs that lead us back to the terracing'. Harmony, magic, enchantment, and balance of shapes and emotions do not follow a single path, and no matter the angle from which they are observed, the beauty and perfection remain the same. The only thing that matters is the emotion within your heart.

At this point you must be tired. Let's go home. I have prepared a simple, but delicious, soup for you with a bizarre name: acquacotta (cooked water). I diced plenty of onions and sautéed them with a touch of oil in a stone pot until they reached a beautiful golden brown, paying special attention to not overcook them before adding a deep red tomato from the garden. I cut a potato into large pieces and, coupled with a bit of chicory, I added them to the pot with a pinch of salt and just enough water necessary to let it all simmer until cooked. The slices of stale bread are carefully placed along the rim of the bowl, ready to welcome the vegetable broth, and with the small amount left in the pot I crack an egg and cover it for just a few moments until a light white veil conceals the mysterious yellow colour of the yoke. The recipe is complete when the egg is added to the vegetables along with a splash of olive oil, having the green colour of hope, the same as that which is within me in the hope that you were impressed with our extraordinary walk to Villa Lante".

The local guide of Viterbo may dissolve and disappear in the depths of our imagination, but the description of the beauty vibrantly remains in our memories.

Spas

At the end of a long walk, the need to relax both the mind and body is only natural while remaining wrapped up in the local charm. With its fantastic spas and steam rooms, Viterbo provides the perfect opportunity to relish in the desires of relaxation.

The spa has two main establishments designed with a modern and captivating style. Beginning with the ancient Romans, the healing properties of these waters attract passionate tourists to the two most popular establishments including Terme dei Papi di Viterbo with its Hotel Niccolo V, as well as to the Salus Terme with its Hotel Benessere and Spa.

For anyone looking to dive into nature, there are also free hot springs (Piscine Carletti and Bullicame) where you can have a swim in the hot thermal waters free of charge. The most surprising aspect of this area is its microclimate, which creates a halo of mysterious vapours that allow you to take advantage of these beneficial springs even during the winter months. Also worth mentioning are two other natural, outdoor pools in the countryside which are easily reached from the Via Martana and the Via Castigliane. Currently managed by an association, entry requires a membership pass (www.bagnaccio.it), which includes access to various springs, hyperthermal baths (65-66 degrees Celcius) and hypothermal baths (23-29 degrees Celcius).

Otherwise, there are the Masse di S. Sisto thermal baths in the southern part of Cassia toward the direction of Rome about 7 km from the centre of Viterbo. Similar to those mentioned above, a membership grants access to its thermal baths.

In conclusion, for those who wish to have some fun while in the company of culture and nature, and to organize a perfect spa weekend, this is the right place: high quality and friendly hospitality for any budget.

Cultural and Religious Events

Viterbo stands out as a place worth discovering, and should you happen upon it during the summer you are sure to bear witness to one of the most unique events in the world: the transport of the Macchina of Santa Rosa. This quintessential celebration is dedicated to the patron saint of the city of Viterbo, Santa Rosa of the 13th century. The "macchina" of Santa Rosa consists of a large metal tower, about 3o metres tall and weighing about 5 tonnes. The tower is constructed and embellished with various types of materials, and is illuminated by torches and electric bulbs. Every year, on the evening of the 3rd of September, the impressive structure is hoisted on the shoulders of about one hundred of the cities most robust men, known as "facchini", or porters, and carried for about 1 km through the narrow streets of the medieval town centre amongst the praise and rapture of the crowd.

We can now move on to southern Lazio, not far from Rome and near Latina, for a visit amidst history and nature.

The Caetani Castle
Upon a hill about 250 metres above sea level, rows of houses surround the large castle of a small village. Beginning in the 13th century, the castle once belonged to the Annibaldi family, a noble dynasty from Rome, who also owned Ninfa and the castles of Bassiano, San Donato and Sermoneta, as well as the surrounding territories.

Their domination did not last long, however, before they eventually left their properties to the Caetani family, among which included Pope Bonifacio VIII who negotiated the acquisition process on behalf of his nephew Pietro II, count of Caserta. In 1297, reign over Sermoneta, Bassiano and San Donato was given to the Caetani family, responsible for revolutionizing the original structure entirely by constructing new internal

49

buildings and commissioning a defensive wall around the castle. At the beginning of the 14th century, under the rule of Giacomo II, the castle became the permanent residence of the Caetani dynasty. During the mid-1400s, Onorato III Caetani slowly began increasing his social, political and military power, which consequently gave way to the golden age of the Sermoneta Empire. Cognizant of this resplendent renaissance, Onorato took this opportunity to build new structures, inviting the most famous artists of the time to fresco both the new and existing rooms. Among these works of art is the so-called "Camere Pinte", frescoed rooms of mythological creatures painted by an unknown artist who was most likely part of the Pinturicchio school.

The territory of Sermoneta has been repeatedly mentioned in ancient manuscripts, indicating that it was already populated in the archaic era. The ancient Volscian city of Sulma, mentioned by Virgilio in the Aeneid, was in the same territory of Sermoneta where today stands the Abbey of Valvisciolo.

The "mala aria", or "bad air" felt by increasing expansion of the Pontine Marshes and the continued Saraceni invasions eventually forced residents of the ancient city of Sulmo to move to today's Sermoneta, already named so in the 11th century.

By exploiting the advantageous position of Sermoneta along the Via Pedemontana, the enterprising Caetani family turned the city in the centre of dominance of southern Lazio. In order to defend this power and to continue capitalizing on the many advantages of this important road which replaced the Via Appia in connecting northern and southern Italy, the residents of Sermoneta fought against the residents of nearby Ninfa, eventually conquering the city before turning their attention to the neighbouring city of Sezze. It was during this period of great success that the construction of residential buildings in the medieval town began, and still stands perfectly intact today. The rising power of the Cateani, however, came to end in 1499 when Alessandro VI Borgia excommunicated the family and revoked their property, privileges, and rights with a public decree issued by the Pope. Under the Borgia reign, the castle was used as a military fort. Consequentially, the castle walls were reinforced, the last floor of the tower was destroyed, and the church of San Pietro in Corte was reduced to rubble without any respect for the remains of the Caetani family members who had been buried there since the 1400. The castle became so impenetrable that in 1536 Charles V failed miserably in his attempt to storm the castle despite the force of a thousand horses and four thousand soldiers.

Nevertheless, the power of the Borgia reign was short-lived, and in 1504 Pope Julius II reinstated the Caetani family as the lords of Sermoneta.

In the 16th century, recovery efforts of the Pontine Marshes began in order to re-open the Via Appia. This endeavour eventually led to the slow, but steady decline of Sermoneta, and in 1567 it lost its title as the "capital of the Caetani dukedom" to Cisterna.

Following the Second World War, thanks to the reclamation of the territory of the Pontine Marshes, the city centre was abandoned and residents were able to relocate to the lowlands where the small towns of Doganella, Tufette, Pontenuovo, and Carrara, on the border with the Cisterna Municipality of Latina and Latina, emerged.

The beautiful borough of Sermoneta, along with its rich history, has made it a magnet for tourism.

How to get there

By train: the Rome-Naples line, with both regional and intercity trains, connects Rome to the Latina Scalo station in about 30-35 minutes (from Naples, a 90-minute intercity train). A bus leaving from the piazza just outside the train station or from the other side of the overpass, to the left of the station (for bus times, ask for information), will take you to the entrance of the city of Sermoneta. Taxi services can also be found in the piazza of the train station (Tel. +39 0773-632292).

By car or coach: along the Via Appia, at the crossroad for Latina Scalo, taking the road that leads to the train station, go beyond the overpass of the railroad tracks and follow indications for Sermoneta. Parking is available outside of the city walls.

By bike: Bikes are allowed on all regional trains. The 10 km route from the Latina Scalo station consists of a difficult incline.

Itinerary

The charity "Roffredo Caetani", established by Lelia, the last descendent of the Caetani family, and her husband Hubert Howard, was established in order to preserve the family riches, and to promote cultural activities in appreciation of the heritage within the antique halls of the castle.

The most fulfilling way to visit the castle is to book a tour guide who will take you on a captivating journey, capable of reliving the history of the castle along with the mix of emotions evoked by the past. The tour begins in the Piazza d'Armi and crosses the first two draw bridges which lead you to a large courtyard surrounded by the castle walls, the Maschio tower and the noblemen's palaces. Here, you will find yourself immersed in the historical landmarks that highlight life within the castle. From there, the tour leads to a visit of the "Casa del Cardinale", where visitors can admire the paintings, elegant furniture and Ninfa frescoes of the only structure inhabited and built during the Borgiana era. A stairway leads to a two-story building from the

1400s where grain was produced, as well as to the stables with vaulted ceilings. Crossing the Piazza d'Armi a second time, and after a short visit to the various bedrooms, known as "Camere Pinte", named after the 15th century frescoes, the tour then takes visitors to the "Sala dei Baroni", where parties and banquets were held. Exiting from the hallway, and passing by the servants' quarters, visitors then return to the courtyard to reach the kitchen where the ancient hood of the chimney towers over the courtyard.

Defense structures, including the castle wall walk and the Maschio and Maschietto towers, which are accessible by crossing the third draw bridge, are also worth visiting. Aside from being used as defensive structures, both towers were at times used as the lord's residence. On the first floor of the Maschio tower is a perfectly preserved bedroom furnished in 16th century furniture. From these bedrooms, visitors then cross a fourth draw bridge and walk along the exterior wall where soldiers once patrolled the crenelated fortifications of the Borgia era. The final part of the tour consists of a walk through a tunnel which leads to the second draw bridge adjacent to the Piazza d'Armi, also known as the "lunga batteria".

It comes as no surprise that this part of Italy provided the set of the beautiful film "Tale of Tales" by Garrone, who filmed a few scenes from the story of "The Old Woman Who Was Skinned" set in the Caetani Castle of Sermoneta and shows a part of the fortress which is closed to the public, the stables, and the wall walk, with Vincent Cassel as the leading protagonist. Scenes from the fantastic film, "Non ci resta che piangere", or "Nothing Left to Do but Cry" by Roberto Benigni and Massimo Troisi were also filmed in the stables.

The tour consists of a single route of about 60 minutes, and is always given in groups accompanied by an official tour guide. The route is quite demanding and people with mobility difficulties are discouraged from doing it.

It is possible to visit the Castle of Sermoneta and the Ninfa Gardens, belonging to the Roffredo Caetani Foundation, within a day by dedicating half a day to each.

Opening Hours: Every day except Thursday; in the morning from 10am-12pm; 2pm-4pm from October to March, and from 3pm-6pm from April to September (Please note: 2pm-4pm on Monday and Wednesday during the months of April and May). For more information and reservations (required for groups), please call +39 0773-30008.

For information about tours, visit: www.fondazionecaetani.org.

The Surrounding Areas
of the Caetani Castle and Sermoneta

The areas surrounding Sermoneta provide opportunities to visit places of great historical, architectural, and naturalistic importance. For example, the ancient hamlet and gardens of Ninfa (7.2 km from Sermoneta) are easily included in the same trip to Sermoneta and the Caetani castle. Another option could be the ancient city of Norba, a short distance from Norma (10.5 km from Sermoneta), perched above a cliff overlooking the Pontine Marshes. A visit to the Abbey of Valvisciolo is a must as it is an important example of the Gothic-Cistercian style, where art, history and mystery form a perfect union of nobility. This cherished place is by far one of the most visited in all of Lazio and merits an in-depth visit.

Further south, near Montecassino, is a city well-known for its history but unrecognizable by name.

Entering from the eastern side of the city, visitors find themselves in front of an engraving on the Porta Napoli, which recounts important traces of centuries worth of the city's history: *"Oh wayfarer, you are now entering Arpino, founded by Saturn, city of the Volschi, municipality of the Romans, hometown of Marco Tullio Cicerone, prince of eloquence, and of Caio Mario, seven-term consul. From this place, the triumphant eagle took flight towards the empire and brought the world under the wings of Rome. Recognize its prestige and live long"*. These are the words engraved at the entrance of the city, placing emphasis on the cultural context and giving life to the history of Arpino.

True understanding and discovery of the beauty of a new place means wandering and returning home more enriched than when you left. A traveller is in search of surprises, and as Mario Soldati so eloquently stated, a journey begins first and foremost with a feeling before becoming reality. Visiting Arpino is an emotional experience that cannot be reproduced, not only for its enchanting landscapes and natural beauties that can be enjoyed in this small, hillside town wedged between Abruzzo, Campania and Molise, but also for its alluring historical traditions that emerge from its monuments and works of art scattered throughout the city. Home to well-known artists, Arpino is situated near the National Park of Abruzzo, Molise, Campania, the Nature Reserve of Posta Fibreno Lake, the path of the Liri river, the waterfalls of the Island of Liri, the Abbey of Casamari and the Abbey of Montecassino.

A Bit of History

In the hometown of Cicerone, Caio Mario, Vipsanio Agrippa, Giuseppe Cesari and San Francesco Saverio Maria Bianchi, history consists of a series of infinite paths, each one distinct, yet connected, by a nexus, at times indiscernible, which cultivates our modern world.

Arpino is a small town upon a hill about 450 metres above sea level, in the province of Frosinone, and is home to about 7500 residents. The small, yet historically significant, town was home to several well-known men of history: Caio Mario (159 – 86 B.C.), a General and a Roman politician, proclaimed the founder of Rome after Romolo and Camillo, and the ambassador for seven terms; Marco Tullio Cicerone (106 – 43 B.C.), a famous public speaker, statesman, philosopher and scholar of ancient literature, known for his numerous literary productions; Marco Vipsanio Agrippa (63 – 12 B.C.) the architect of the Pantheon in Rome; Giuseppe Cesari (1568 – 1635), a famous painter from the 1600s *"pictur unicus, rarus et excellens ac primarius et reputatus"*, and teacher of Caravaggio.

Among the many prominent figures, also worth mentioning is Pasquale Rotondi (1909-1991), director of the Central Institute of Restoration, and known for having saved nearly ten-thousand pieces of art from theft and destruction by the Nazis during WWII. Rotondi's diary kept during the operation has been made into a book titled "L'arca dell'arte", edited by Salvatore Giannella and Pier Damiano Mandelli, and has also been recreated in a film titled "La lista di Pasquale Rotondi", produced by Rai Educational (a broadcasting TV station which aims to promote education and culture).

According to the legend, Saturn, the mythological god responsible for the protection of crops and whose reign was depicted as the Golden Age, founded the city of Arpino. Fragments of his tomb still remain in the so called "Jocca 're ll'Ova", a tomb where, according to an Arpinian historian named Clavelli, Saturn's ashes can be found along with the engraving: *"Conditur hic primus Saturnus morte deorum / Imperio cuius Arpinium fundamina sumpsit"*.

Traditions passed from one generation to the next describe the city's first residents as the Pelasgi, a pre-Hellenic population believed to have built the megalithic walls, known as the "pelasgiche". More credibly, the so-called city of Cicerone, was under the rule of the Volsci in the 7th century B.C., and then of Samnites in the 4th century B.C. At the end of the 3rd century B.C., Arpino came under Roman rule, gaining Roman suffrage in 188 B.C. In the Middle Ages, Arpino was the centre of many major events as part of the Roman duchy, and was later passed to the Longobardi dynasty.

In 787, Arpino was donated to the papacy, creating a motive of conflict between the Catholic Church and the Roman Empire. The city was occupied by the Normanni and by Frederick II, who destroyed the city in 1229. Throughout the 13th century, it was controlled by the Svevi, and later by the Angevin dynasty. In fact, the Civit Falconara Castle was built in this era and at the beginning of the 1400's, the King of Naples, Ladislao d'Angiò of Durazzo, transformed the castle into a palace. Today, the palace is noted as Ladislao Castle where the Umberto Mastroianni Foundation is housed, along with the simple tower of Civitavecchia that emerges from the highest point of the two hills on which Cicerone is situated.

The tower, erroneously named after Cicerone due to the widespread belief during the Middle Ages that Civitavecchia of Arpino was the home of the celebrated orator, along with the tower of Montenero and Santopadre, were designated watch towers for Arpino.

The castle and tower constitute the hinge that encloses the powerful fortification systems of Arpino, and of which the initial nucleus, composed of cyclopean walls, was brought back by the scholars of the 7th century B.C. During the medieval period, the Longobardi and the Franchi used it as a fortified wall, reinforcing it with more towers, which are still intact today. The megalithic walls of Arpino, with its pointed arch, have the longest and most preserved perimeter (about 3 km) in Italy. In 1580, Arpino became part of the Sora duchy; in 1796 the territory of Arpino was annexed to the Kingdom of Naples and between the 17th and 18th centuries it experienced extraordinary economic and demographic development thanks to the manufacturing of wool, making it well known in many parts of Europe. It was later designated to the Kingdom of Sicily until 1860, to the province of Terra di Lavoro until 1927, and finally to the province of Frosinone.

PART TWO

ABRUZZO

The discrete charm of Arpino harbours an ancient past that has persisted throughout the ages, much of which is still observable today. One example of its ancient past is Civitavecchia, an acropolis considered by archaeologists to be the original centre of the very first Volschi settlements. Surrounding this acropolis are menacing polygonal walls, thought to be one of the most well kept wall structures of the pre-Roman area.

Of particular significance is the "arco a sesto acuto", or the pointed archway whose structure archaeologists attribute to the Tiryns and Mycenae, and is the only arch of its type in the entire Mediterranean.

Three monuments remain in the acropolis: the so-called "torre di Cicerone", the San Vito church of the 17th-18th century, characterized by three naves reworked in a modern style and a 1625-1627 altarpiece by Giuseppe Cesari, known as "il Cavalier d'Aprino", or "the Hero of Arpino", which represent the saints Vitus, Modestus and Crescentia.

Next to the "arco a sesto acuto" stands the small Santissima Trinità church, otherwise known as the Crucified Simulacrum, designed in the classic Roman style in a Greek cross. Founded in 1720, the church has a late-Baroque style façade with statues sculpted by Michele Stolz.

Strolling along the city streets, sitting in the piazza Municipio, or climbing the small steps of a modern-day Arpino, successions of aristocratic palaces rich with works of art and history are waiting to be discovered in every corner.

The Churches
When looking at history through an artistic and cultural lens, monuments begin to symbolize a primary objective on behalf of civilization, along with an effort to give intellectual significance to everything we humans have in common. When traveling through the city of Arpino, it is easy to find copious amounts of architecturally exquisite churches and sanctuaries that safeguard works of enormous artistic value, a few of which are described below.

The Saint Mary church of Loreto al Castello was constructed in the 18th century atop the ruins of the polygonal tower of the city walls. The church has an octagonal apse which contains two Cassevano frescoes representing the transfer of the painting of the Madonna of Loreto of the

San Sebastian church and a group of Franciscan monks. On the central altar is an admirable and well-preserved painting of the Santa Casa being transported by angels.

The Saint Roch church was built in the 17th century on one of the two large towers of the city walls. Inside the church, on a small marble altar, a small statue of the idolized saint celebrated on the 16th of August, is protected in a display case. The church also has two small frescos on each side of the altar.

The Santa Maria of Civita church has a history that can only be partially reconstructed by a scarce amount of epigraphic documentaries. The church is designed with three naves in a Latin cross, and protects cherished paintings by Cavalier d'Arpino. The only remains of the Roman era is the decoration on the polygonal blocks of the bell tower and two headstones that represent, respectively, the reconstruction of the towers by the consul Gnaeus Acerronius Proculus and the restoration of the temple by three builders. The painting of Saint Jerome originated from the school of Caravaggio. However, Saint James, the Annunciation of the Lord, and Saint Joseph's Dream are paintings of the 18th century Roman school. At the entrance of the church, an inscription recalls a visit by Charles III of Spain in 1749. The church was remodelled in a late-Baroque style at the end of the 18th century, and more recently throughout the 19th century.

The structure of the Santa Maria delle Grazie church reflects 17th century standards of design and underwent restoration in the 19th century. A treaty between Pope Pius II, the Aragonese people and the Angevins is also believed to have been signed in this small church in 1463 with the following testimony: *"in Ecclesiae Sanctae Mariae Graziarum extra muros terre Arpini"*.

The Saint Michael the Archangel church was constructed in the area of a Pagan temple dedicated to Apollo and the Muses. Notable works by Cavalier d'Arpino are protected within the church. The Baroque-style interior is designed in the shape of a Latin cross, with three naves with lateral chapels. On the main altar, a canvas painting of Saint Michael the Archangel dominates the space and a painting of the Eternal Father is depicted on the vault of the apse, both of which were done by Cavalier d'Arpino, just like the Annunciation, Tobias and the Angel, the martyrdom of Saint Peter and the Station of the Cross. Of particular value is the Station of the Cross of the Tuscan school of the 14th century depicted on the right nave, the painting of the Virgin and Child by the 17th century painter Dionigi Ludovisi and, in the sacristy, the painting from the Caravaggio school attributed to Francesco Cairo representing the baptism of Jesus. The wooden furnishings, the baptistery and the pulpit are all works by the sculptor Michele Stolz (1725-1779), whereas the organ was made by Cesare Catarinozzi of Subiaco in 1721.

The 18th century SS Carlo and Filippo Church was annexed to the San Carlo College, entrusted by Desiderio Merolle to the Barnabite priests. Today, however, the church has been deconsecrated.

Presently deconsecrated, the Church of the Holy Cross from the 17th century was built next to the monastery of Cappuccinelle, and was at one time the seat of the Tulliano College.

The Church of the Pietà, dating back to the 16th century, contains a fresco from the 17th century. Each year, the solemn procession leaves from this church and crosses the streets of the city on Holy Friday.

Dating back to the 1300s, the Church of San Antonio is considered to be the oldest confraternity in Arpino and has been considered its oldest church since 1622. Following an earthquake in 1654, the church was rebuilt, and underwent a restoration process in 1727 when the church was re-consecrated. Since then, the church has maintained its Baroque style. Of notable importance and beauty within the church is the painted canvas of the dressing of Saint Anthony by Cavalier d'Arpino and the crucifix sculpted by Stolz. Also worth noting is the decoration of the nave and of the presbytery by the Neapolitan school dating back to the 1700s.

Located in Civitavecchia, the Romanesque style church of Santissima Trinità is designed in a Greek cross, and was built in 1720 by Cardinal

Giuseppe Pesce, rector of the Papal Chapel. Also found in the church are works by Stolz, including the statue of the Immaculate Conception and the Crucifix.

The Church of San Vito in Civitavecchia is of the 16th century and is designed with three naves. Saint Vitus, Crescentia, and Modestus by Cavalier d'Arpino and a statue of Saint Vitus by Michele Stolz are depicted inside the church.

Knowledge of the church of Saint Andrew dates back to 1084. The church was destroyed and reconstructed throughout the 13th century, undergoing further renovations and structural changes, with the most substantial changes taking place in 1533 and 1780. Next to the church sits the ancient cloistered Benedictine convent founded in the 6th century by Saint Scholastica. The statue of the Assumption of Mary, protector of Arpino since 1802, is enshrined in the church. The baptistery, sculpted by Federico Tretter in 1782, as well as the 18th century organ, is also of great beauty to be admired in this ancient church.

According to 13th century manuscripts (Rationes decimarum), the San Sebastian church was built between 1308 and 1310, and was considered property of the Montecassino monastery. In 1797, the church was used as a hospital for people suffering from leprosy, and in 1915 endured serious structural damage due to the earthquake in Marsica, but luckily, the apse frescoes were saved. Major internal restoration in 1981 allowed for the series of frescoes to be admired, including Saint Dominic by Guzman and San Sebastian with the city of Ambrogio of Ferentino in the background, painted in 1498. At the base of the painting, an inscription reads *"Opus Ambrosii Ferentinatis Anno Domini 1498 mense augusti die octavio"*, establishing the indisputable origin and date of the painting. The painting of San Sebastian shooting an arrow, on the other hand, dates back to the 18th century. The bust of the Nursing Madonna and the painted canvas of the Martyrdom of Saint Sebastian are also of great worth inside the church.

Museums and Cultural Events

History can be thought of as a mirror that reflects the many achievements of mankind. Therefore, looking to the past can help us make sense of the present. Our understanding of our own world depends on our intention to share that knowledge with the rest of the world. The ability to share it, however, is strongly connected to our cultural heritage. This is why our historical heritage must be valued and maintained through various initiatives. With this idea in mind, the hometown of Cicerone has worked to create museums, charities and cultural events to protect its cultural heritage for generations to come. Dedicated to one of the greatest artists of the 1900s, the "Mastroianni" Foundation is considered one of the most important cultural institutions of the city. The Museum of the Industrial Archaeology of Wool, which bears witness to the history of the economic development in the area of Ciociaria, displays and preserves the equipment and machinery of the antique Diodati wool mills. The Stringed Instrument Museum gives testimony to the glorious musical tradition of the city of Arpino, and includes the artisanal workshop of the stringed instruments handcrafted by the maestros Embergher and his pupil Cerrone dating back to the 1880. Another citywide project known as the Libro di Pietra, or Stone Book, created by Giuseppe Bonaviri in 1983, aims to commemorate various poets by reproducing literary works dedicated to Arpino by contemporary artists on slabs of marble displayed throughout the city. The "Certamen Ciceronianum" is a cultural event of European significance, which memorializes the work of Cicerone.

The Remains of the Via Latina
Initially beginning in Rome and continuing south toward the original "lega latina" cities through Ferentino, Frosinone, Ceprano, Aquino, Cassino, Teano and Santa Maria Capua Vetere, the Via Latina has existed since the 4th century B.C. and used to unite Rome and Ceprano (the old Fregellae), and as a result crossed the Samnites territory in order to control the surrounding areas. The Via Latina was one of the three most

important Roman roads of communication (Appia, Valeria, Latina) and was directed toward Arpino after crossing the bridge of Saint Paul. Traces of the ancient Via Latina in Arpino are still visible today near the train station and consist of a whole segment of stone which functions as a traffic divider. According to the experts, the Via Latina continued toward Arpino, flanking the church of Saint Sebastian and the church of the Madonna of the Consolazione, where at one time a tunnel led inside the city walls (the exit was next to the defensive tour where the sacristy of the church of San Rocco appears).

Food and Wine

The culinary traditions of Arpino feature various dishes, among which include: "sagna e fagioli" (pasta and beans), "fettuccine con funghi porcini, pancetta e asparagi" (fettuccine pasta with porcini mushrooms, pancetta, and asparagus), "fettuccine al tartufo" (fettuccine pasta with truffle oil), "minestra con cotiche, fagioli, verdura e salsicce" (pork rind, beans, vegetables and sausage soup), "polenta e spuntature di maiale" (polenta with pork spare ribs), "abbacchio alla brace" (grilled lamb), "capozzella (testa) di abbachhio con le patate al forno" (lamb's head with oven roasted potatoes), "spezzatino di pecora" (stewed mutton), "pecorino e ricottine fesche con verdure e tartufo" (goat cheese and fresh ricotta with vegetables and truffle). Among the desserts which stand out are: "crostate di ricotta" (ricotta tart), "pigna ricresciuta con uvetta e frutta candida" (cake made with raisins and candied fruit), "mostaccioli al cioccolato e marmellata" (chocolate and marmalade pasta), and finally, "torroncini di pasta reale" (nougat candy).

A Simple Recipe: Sagne e Fagioli
(Pasta and Beans)
Ingredients: flour, Cannellini beans, olive oil, onion, garlic, red pepper flakes, celery, salt (if desired, cubes of pancetta and tomato sauce can also be added)
Directions: Knead the flour (whole grain flour is also acceptable) with the amount of water necessary to obtain malleable dough. Knead the dough for a few minutes, and flatten with a rolling pin in order to have a very thin, round layer of pastry. Roll the pastry, and with a sharp knife cut the dough into medium-sized shapes to obtain the so-called "maltagliati" or "badly cut" pasta. Toss the pasta with your fingers in order to separate the individual pieces. Cook in salted water and remove the pasta from the stove when it becomes yellow. Drain the pasta, leaving a bit of water in the pot. Flavour the boiled beans with a simple sauce made by browning the onions, garlic, celery, the cubes of pancetta and tomato sauce (if desired), and red pepper flakes or black pepper to add a bit of spice. Combine the pasta with the sauce, mix, and serve.

How to get there

Arpino is about 3o km from Frosinone and is equidistant from Rome and Naples (about 120 km). Arpino is also easily reached from Abruzzo and from the Adriatic side of Italy. The Abruzzo National Park, Lazio, and Molise, the Nature Reserve of Posta Fibreno Lake, the Casamari Abbey and the Abbey of Montecassino are also accessible from Arpino.

From Naples:

By train: the Roccasecca stop on the Naples-Rome train line (via Cassino); the Arpino stop on the Roccasecca-Avezzano train line.

By car: A1 highway Naples-Milan, Cassino exit. Cassino highway toward Sora, Arpino exit. Otherwise, the A1 highway (Milan-Naples), exit Ceprano. Follow indications for Arce-Sora until reaching the SS82 of the Valle dei Liri (about 6 km). Follow the road for 7 km toward Sora, until reaching the crossroad for Arpino.

By bus: CO.TRA.L. – CIALONE.

From Rome:

By train: the Frosinone stop on the Rome-Naples train line (via Cassino). From there, bus CO.TRA.L. towards Sora, Isola Liri. Once in Sora, bus CO.TRA.L toward Arpino.

By car: A1 highway (Milano-Naples), exit Ferentino. From there, take the highway from

Frosinone-Sora exit Castelliri (15 km). From there, follow indications for Arpino (about 10 km).

By bus: CO.TRA.L. – CIALONE.

<u>From the Adriatic side</u>:

By car: A24 highway (Rome-Teramo) and A25 (Rome-Pescara), exit Avezzano. Take the Avezzano-Sora-Cassino highway, exit Broccostella, and follow the indications (about 9 km).

Itinerary

Among the main attractions of Arpino are the Cammino of San Benedetto, the waterfalls of the Isle of Liri, the San Domenico Abbey in Sora, Piazza Municipio, Civitavecchia and the gorges of Melfa in Arpino are all worth visiting. For information: Proloco (Grass-roots organizations seeking to promote the city), call +39 0776-848535.

Otherwise, tours on horseback in the mountains of Ciociaria are also available. For information, call +39 320-0533604.

PART THREE

TUSCANY

Reggello
and the Castle of Sammezzano

It is never difficult to come up with a valid excuse to visit the world-famous rolling hills of Tuscany. However, for once it would be nice to go on a new kind of adventure to discover its unknown parts, which are nevertheless beautiful and alluring. Home to Dante Alighieri, Michelangelo, Giotto and many other famous artists, anyone who visits Tuscany will find himself or herself under its spell, and may even decide to settle there.

The area of Reggello is near the part of Florence where Garrone managed to track down an astonishing castle. While difficult to visit, the castle warrants particular time and attention, and stands little chance at survival without an increase in touristic demand.

Sometimes, beautiful things are much closer than we ever realize. And yet, because of our frenetic routines of daily life, we do not always appreciate what we have around us. One of the most magnificent places included in the beauty of the hidden parts of Italy, which exemplifies the definition of Italian excellence, can be reached by following the A1 highway between Florence and Rome. Slightly before reaching the exit for Incisa-Reggello, a castle emerges on the left from a forested hillside: the Castle of Sammezzano.

Garrone chose to shoot a few scenes of the story of Cassel, king of Roccaforte, in this small castle. Located in the municipality of Reggello (FI), the Sammezzano Castle is privately owned, and only occasionally opens to the public.

Once known as Castelvecchio di Cascia, Reggello originally functioned as a marketplace between the Via of Casentino and Cassia Vetus (known today as the "strada dei Setteponti" or "the road of seven bridges"). The municipality of Reggello was established in 1773 following a legislative measure taken by Leopold II, Grand Duke of Tuscany. During an 1860 referendum to unite Tuscany with Sardegna, many vote holders were extremely opposed to the annexation, which lead to record breaking levels of abstention (971 votes cast out of 2899) at the time of voting, causing the measure to fail.

From 1970 to 1990, the Sammezzano Castle functioned as a rather famous and important hotel and restaurant. Following its closure in 1990, however, it remained closed after a series of misfortunes, and was eventually bought by an English-Italian association in hopes of reviving the castle and recreating a 5-star hotel and golf course. For the time being, the project has been brushed aside, however the castle is once again accessible on certain days of the year thanks to a committee of volunteers (www.sammezzano.org) whose tours have brought to light the urgency of restoration and maintenance.

The committee was established in 2012 in celebration of the life of Ferdinando Panciatichi Ximenes d'Aragona (Florence, 10 March 1813 – Sammezzano, 18 October 1897), owner and project designer of the castle. Ferdinando spent nearly fifty years working to build his "Oriental Dream". It could therefore be said that the life of Ferdiando and Sammezzano existed as one, making anyone who entered or returned to this man-made wonder truly fortunate.

Ferdinando's knowledge and accomplishments represent the essence of a true Renaissance man. Fluent in many languages including Italian, French, English, Spanish, several oriental languages, and ancient Latin and Greek, he was also an honorary member of the Commission of Architects and Engineers of Florence, a botanist, an avid reader, an entrepreneur, and a multifaceted intellectual. He raised money and collaborated with various cultural institutions of Florence including the Accademia di Belle Arti, the Museum of the Bargello, the Uffizi, the Accademia of Georgofili and the Tuscan Society of Horticulture. Part of his personal archives was donated to the National Archive of Italy in 1888. Ferdinando was also an open-minded and patriotic person who was a member of parliament in the Kingdom of Italy from 1864-1867. In order to provide an even deeper understanding of this well-rounded public figure, an inscription in one room of the castle reads:

PUDET DICERE SED VERUM EST:
PUBLICANI SCORTA LATRONES ET
PROXENATAE ITALIAM CAPIUNT
VORANTQUE NEC NE HOC DOLEO
SED QUIA MALA OMNIA NOS
MERUISSE CENSEO

translated as *"I am ashamed to say it, but it is true: debt collectors, harlots, thieves, and businessmen hold Italy in the palm of their hand and they are devouring it, yet what truly causes me grievance is the fact that we deserve it"*. The statement still rings so true today that it is almost as if time was frozen at the very moment of its engraving. At any rate, only a person with Ferdinando's character could have built a magical place like Sammezzano, a place that literally allows visitors to "escape" to China, Saudi Arabia, Persia, India, or Spain. Each room is more beautiful than the next (falsely identified as 365 rooms by poorly informed writers). Certain rooms are particularly studied, such as the ballroom illuminated in a dazzling white colour (resembling the Alhambra of Granada), and the Peacock Room, which evokes images of Moghul art forms and has become an object of true devotion all over the world. The rooms of the castle were all inspired by some of the most beautiful and iconic places in the world, places where Ferdinando never had the chance to visit. His travel experiences were limited to Europe (primarily London and Paris to visit the first world's fair, as well as Monaco and Antwerp), however records indicate that he never travelled to Asia or Spain. As he travelled, he purchased precious and beautiful books, deeply studying them and reproducing the immense sense of culture in Sammezzano with everything being created on-site exclusively by Tuscan labour.

Can anyone else in the world say that they had the good fortune or privilege of thinking, planning, financing, and building their own ideal world? The city of Sammezzano, however, is made up of more than just architecture and colour. It is complete with history, politics, esotericism and symbolism. In addition to being a blend of many cultures, it is also a park. On the nearly fifty hectares of historical park surrounding the castle, Ferdinando planted more than 180 types of exotic plants. While many died, others survived, such as the very first Sequoya tree Ferdinando bought in 1864 for 224 lire, much to the scandal of the general population. Today, the Park of Sammezzano has the largest concentration of Sequoya trees in Europe, and also houses the "twin Redwood", a 50-meter tree with a nearly nine meter circumference which is included in the strict category of the "150 Most Important Trees in Italy".

To quote Ferdinando's words found in the entrance hall of the castle, Sammezzano is a "non plus ultra", a place to be visited, but most of all to be saved.

As mentioned above, the castle is located in Reggello, a sweeping (121 km/sq) municipality in the province of Florence that extends from the Arno River to Monte Secchieta (1, 200 m). On the more elevated ground, the Vallombrosa and Sant'Antonio forests make up an area of 2,000 hectares. Along the beautiful ancient road "via dei setteponti" or the "road of seven bridges" which connects Fiesole and Arezzo, ancient olive groves and breath-taking landscapes are typical features of the natural scenery for which Florence is famous. Below the olive groves, another naturalistic area awaits. Known as "le Balze", or "pleated cliffs", the characteristic rock face was at one time part of a lake bottom, which eventually dried out. Under the cliffs are 180 hectares of woodlands (holly oak, poison oak, etc.) with 50 hectares of historical park, all of which makes up the Park of Sammezzano. And, last but not least, the Arno River.

Once the decision to visit the territory of Reggello has been made, it is absolutely necessary to visit the Abbey of Vallombrosa, situated in a forest beautifully manicured by the monks of Saint Giovanni Gualberto, protector of the

Italian foresters. Take plenty of time to relish in the peace and quiet of Vallombrosa, especially during the off-season periods of the year, perhaps accompanied by a monk who is sure to make anyone fall in love with this timeless place.

Returning to the Incisa-Reggello entrance to the A1 highway and exiting at Reggello, a church known as Pieve di Cascia justifies a trip to this area of Tuscany all on its own. After taking a closer look, a "small" but very precious museum possesses an authentic jewel: the San Giovenale Triptych, the earliest known work by the extraordinary genius, born Tommaso Cassai, but known world-wide as Masaccio. Massimo Sottani, former mayor of Reggello and active member of the committee working to protect the Castle of Sammezzano, said it best: "Believe me, seeing the painting and listening to the explanation by Don Dailli is just as valuable as an entire day at the Uffizi".

Food and Wine

It is not by chance that Reggello is home to the oldest review of extra virgin olive oil. For years, the best olive oil in Florence has been the "olive oil of Reggello". It is so delicious that the inhabitants of Reggello celebrate it with the "Extra Virgin Olive Oil Festival". Exhibition stands of attending agricultural businesses offer tastings of their latest oil accompanied by some classic bruschetta. The festival takes place around the end of November and ends the 8th of December.

The final day of the festival consists of an "oil race" marathon in the Reggello territory organized by the Resco Reggello Running Association.

Instead of immediately returning to the highway after Reggello, heading toward Leccio at the foot of the Castle of Sammezzano, visitors may wish to do a bit of shopping at "the Mall", perhaps one of the most famous outlet malls in Italy.

As Massimo Sottani stated, "To me, it is more interesting to visit Mario Agostinello (the biggest producer of Zolfini beans in the world)". His beans and his "pink chickpeas" were sampled in 2009 at the G8 Summit in Aquila during a lunch provided by the President of the Republic of Italy.

Good olive oil (from Reggello) and some beans (from Mario) is enough to make you feel like a king.

A Simple but Delicious Recipe: Toasted Bread with Black Cabbage and Zolfini beans

This typical Florentine dish is made exclusively with black cabbage picked after the year's first frost when the cabbage is more tender and sweet. It is prepared with toasted bread sprinkled with garlic, boiled cabbage, salt, and extra virgin olive oil. This simple and tasty dish is typically eaten during the period in which the olives are crushed in Tuscan oil mills (from the site: www.agostinellimario.com).

For information:
www.comune.reggello.fi.it;
www.sammezzano.org;
Sammezzano FPXA committee
Facebook page;
www.monaci.org;
www.museo-masaccio.it;
www.gonnelli1585.it.

Heading back towards the border with Lazio along the coastal area of Tuscany, with the wind at your back as it rustles the leaves of the oak trees, it is easy to embark on the path whose silence is interrupted only by the sound of your own footsteps between the chalky rock walls. The essence of ancient Etruscans, who used to inhabit this space and bury their dead in the famous tomb, surrounds you with every step. Today a touristic destination, the tuff walls, covered in thick layers of moss and other plants, create a sense of mystery and invite discovery. This is known as the so-called "Vie Cave" or "excavated roads".

The Vie Cave of Sovana are ancient Etruscan walking paths that lead to the underlying terrain reaching 25 metres in depth. The topographic arrangement of the path is very unique and merits a visit. It is particularly nice to stop along the path and free the mind while observing the details of the natural landscape. Anyone who chooses to do so will be captivated by the charm and mystery, emphasized by a diffused light that penetrates through the trees and creates a magical world where an ogre could come crashing through the trees at any moment, in chase of the princess in Garrone's film that loosely inspired this book. Or perhaps it is a troop of ancient Roman soldiers making their nightly rounds. After all, you never know! The Vie Cave seem to serve the purpose of connecting the extremely ancient settlements and burial grounds of this area to the uninhabited area of Tuscany between Sovana, Pitigliano and Sorano. While tuff is a rather malleable material to work with, the manually dug roads suggest the immense efforts that went into their creation.

The excavated roads lead to the area of Sovana that at one time was part of the municipality of Sorano. The beauty and unique workings in tuff render these places diamonds in the rough.

The city of Sovana is immersed in a world of green untouched by modern times, and still resembles the same world of the Etruscans who used to call this area *Suf*, or "green earth". The current name of the city itself derives from *Suana*, which is attributed to the Romans after they decided to settle there following the conquest of the territory of Vulci in 278 B.C. Many people recognize the city as the "city of tuff" because of the copious amounts of this material found abandoned in the surrounding areas and consequentially used to construct the majority of the houses in the city.

This small Maremma town is famous for the important monumental tombs and vast burial grounds. In the Middle Ages, the city flourished, as is demonstrated by the various civil and religious buildings that can be admired by taking a walk through the town. As the hometown of Pope Gregory VII, Sovana was the main seat of the bishop and reached its peak in the 13th century when it came under the Aldobrandeschi family. In fact, the Aldobrandeschi Castle, with its defensive tower and surrounding walls highlighting the importance of the city, used to greet visitors of the city at the end of the 11th century. Around the 17th century the castle underwent a strong and steady decline, and today's walls and tower are only partially intact, whereas the entryway made of tuff and equipped with a drawbridge, was completely demolished.

Along the main street there are various palaces to visit, however it is in the Piazza Pretorio that the main monuments can be found, including the Palazzo of the Marquis Bourbon del Monte which has a broad three-arched entryway, and the church of San Mamiliano, built around the 4th century on the remains of an Etruscan and Roman building. In 2004, during restoration efforts of the church, a treasure of nearly 500 gold coins from the 5th century was found and can be seen in the newly rediscovered area and which has now been turned into a museum. Two more monuments that sit in this piazza is the Loggia of the Captain and the Palazzo Pretorio, which also dates back to the 12th-13th century. On the front of Palazzo Pretorio, nine crests represent the captains of justice and successive commissioners during the control of Siena and Florence.

On the western side of the Piazza Pretorio sits the Palazzetto Comunale, also known as the Palazzo of the Archives, with a small covered bell tower.

The cathedral, built in the 11th century and dedicated to Saint Peter and Saint Paul, sits at the edge of town. The cathedral exhibits various architectural styles, including Gothic, Romanesque and Lombard styles, due to the various modifications made over the years.

On the western border with Acquapendente sits the forested town of Sorano, constructed in tuff and nicknamed the Matera of Tuscany for its odd urban planning as a city built into the tuff stone.

Sorano was originally the ancient estate of the Aldobrandeschi family who inhabited this land where important discoveries of Etruscan settlements and burial grounds have been made. As was common during this period, in order to change the fate of the regency, the marriage between Anastasia, the last heir of the Aldobrandeschi dynasty, and Romano Orsini occurred in 1293. From that moment forward, Sorano passed under the control of the Orsini family who resided near Pitigliano, recently considered one of the most beautiful cities in Italy. The required fortifications requested by Count Orsini rendered Sorano a safe refuge from enemy attack. In 1556, Sorano, as well as Pitigliano, came under the control of the Medici family and the Duchy of Tuscany.

Itinerary

The best places to visit include: the Fortezza Orsini; the Porta (Arch) of Ferrini; the Collegiate Church of San Nicola; Masso Leopoldino; the porta of Merli; and the sanctuary of the Madonna of Cerreto.

There are many places around Sorano that deserve a visit. One of these is the "city of tuff" named after the most important rock settlement of central Italy. Represented by more than two hundred caverns, the ancient medieval city of Vitozza was inhabited until the 18th century and carries great historical and cultural value.

Vitozza is a cave settlement dug into the side of a small hill and which was until recently unknown. It can be visited by following a path that begins at San Quirico of Sorano. For many residents, the caverns were simply a shelter for animals or farming equipment.

The golden age of Vitozza was between the 12th and 14th centuries. The walls of the city, the church, and the castle were all built during this time and are found at a higher elevation compared to the caverns. Today, they are easily visible at the top of the hill, surrounded by a few trees and a beautiful lawn. At the time, Vitozza was part of a large empire that included fifteen castles, including Sorano, Pitigliano, Farnese, Mezzano, etc.

The Aldobrandeschi family developed the residential area of the town in the heart of a rocky settlement, most likely inhabited during Etruscan and Roman times. The fortress has two castles: the first castle has thick stone walls that included the entryway; the second castle remains more intact compared to the first, and has a fortified structure along the path leading to the columbaria. To the right of the path that comes from San Quirico, is the "chiesaccia" which consists of the ruins of a medieval church that faces the beautiful woods along the river Lente.

Today, the city of Vitozza, along with the Etruscan burial grounds of Sovana, has been recovered and plays an integral part of the Archaeological Park of the City of Tuff. Its caverns extend along the path of the valley of the Lente River and are important testimonies to the life that once existed in the medieval era.

Within this area are water tanks, reservoirs used to collect waste, various types of niches, drills, curbs for placing bins, and ancient basins carved in rock used since Etruscan and Roman times, and then in the Middle Ages, to produce wine and beer.

The caverns were used for various reasons according necessity, and were subdivided into three categories: a multipurpose cavern used as a residence and animal shelter; stables (recognizable from the presence of troughs and corrals); and caverns used strictly for human habitation (especially present on the southwest side, well-covered and exposed to sunlight). Inside the caverns, grain jars, water wells and chimneys can be found.

From a scenographic point of view, the columbaria made up of many small niches along the walls are a spectacular site. These columbaria were used as funeral monuments during the Roman era, but recently, thanks to the extensive descriptions of ancient scholars, the prevailing hypothesis is that they were used during the Middle Ages as breeding farms for pigeons and doves which is where the name "colombari" comes from. Nature lovers should also visit the water source of the Lente River before leaving the city. You can reach the river via a rather steep and unequipped walking path in the woods.

In addition to the rare beauty of the natural surroundings, bridges as well as the old 19th century aqueduct tunnels, a waterfall, the "ponte del bicchiere" or "glass bridge" and the cavern with the spring will render a visit even more emotional and unforgettable.

After visiting so many enchanting places, it might be a good idea to relax at the nearby hot springs of Saturnia.

These hot springs are known all over the world for their spectacular sulphuric and calcareous waters that have shaped the spring and endowed it with a string of beautiful laced balconies. When they begin to emerge from the last curve of the road that takes you to Saturnia, the hot springs appear like an imaginary scene described by Dante. The steam that wraps around the running water, and flows down splashing against the rocks, creates a magical atmosphere at any time of the day, including at night when illuminated by the moon.

Many people choose to go for a swim after sundown to enjoy the magical romanticism that begins rejuvenating the mind and spirit before even reaching the water.

For the more demanding visitors, there are spa facilities with pools, relaxing sunbeds, and a hotel-restaurant a short distance from the natural hot springs.

When the moment to relax comes to an end, visitors may wish to go toward the amazing beaches in the area. The Natural Uccellina Park is very close to Saturnia. Once again, those who desire more comfort can go to Porto Santo Stefano, Porto Ercole and in the many other resorts nearby, such as Capalbio, a vacation spot frequented by many celebrities.

But it does not end there! The Tarocchi Gardens are also close by. It is an artistic park in Garavicchio, in the surrounding areas of Pescia Fiorentina, a district of Capalbio, designed by a French-American artist Niki de Saint Phalle. The Garden is filled with statues inspired by the arcane figures of Tarocchi.

A few kilometres to the north, you will not only find important archaeological areas such as Vetulonia, but you will also have an opportunity to visit the Abbey of San Galgano whose history is even more captivating thanks to the legend of the "Sword in the Stone". The pyrite found in the mines also deserves a visit, where collectors are sure to find a nugget or two.

The Stars Look Down... on the ancient mining town of Fenice Capanne.

This was the title of a well-known television series in the seventies inspired by A.J. Cronin's novel. The mining shots were taken in the 19th century mining town of Fenice Capanne, located just a few kilometres from Massa Marittima and Lake Accesa.

The deeply rooted history of the mining town dates back to the Etruscans who extracted gold and silver from the shores of the lake where the remnants of ancient settlements can still be found. They also extracted silver from the surrounding wooded areas where vertical mines nearly 80 metres deep still remain. From ancient times to the peak of mining extraction of the 19th century, the small village of Fenice Capanne developed into an urban conglomerate of miners and families, complete with schools, a medical facility, small hotels, and laundries. In the small town, the women worked with copper outside of the mines, while beneath them the men extracted chalcopyrite and copper in deep tunnels nearly 140 metres in depth. The small city centre also had a modest recreational centre, a grocery store, and even a movie theatre. Based on photos dating back to the end of the 1800s, a small church dedicated to Saint Barbara, protector of miners, was also part of the town. Today, the church has been repaired and reopened by volunteers who work to maintain the aspects and characteristics of the original structure. Inside the church is a small mining museum as well as a small mark on the wall, which was revealed in 2013 and is believed to be in memory of the historical priest, Don Luigi, who occupied the church for decades.

The monumental "castelli", a type of lift used by miners that allowed access to the mine, provide testimony to the once flourishing mining activities: the wooden lifts, such as Pozzo Carlo (end of the 19th century), 17 metres high with a vertical structure connected at two points with bolts and plots; the cables of the winch had a flat stone section, such as the Pozzo Salerno (beginning of the 20th century); a two-story stone tower with arched openings; and the Pozzo Costantino, placed within a unique building.

A few other known aspects of Tuscany include the archaeological mining town, framed by Maremma landscapes and enchanting trails that offer an alternative touristic experience and whose primary theme centres on rediscovering the traces of activities surrounding mining extraction.

To this day, Fenice Capanne is wrapped in a halo of mystery, immersed in the untouched nature of the Tuscan Maremma, with unique and exceptional places accessible by foot, by bike, or on horseback similar to the Yellow Desert or the Grand Canyon, characterized by striking colours and landscapes caused by the remains of the extraction of minerals, not to mention Serra Bottini, the powder keg and the woods of the Nonni, and last but not least the Accesa Lake.

The Accesa Lake was originally an underground river, 45 metres deep and awarded five sails by the Guida Blu of Legambiente and Touring Club in 2009. Various legends have been passed down through the years, such as the curse of Saint Anne, patron of the harvest, or that of Birillo the crocodile. According to the legend, during the celebration of Saint Anne, on the 26th of July, people heard the bellowing cries of the oxen and farmers who had been swallowed up by the fields where they were working, instead of honouring the day dedicated to the saint. It is said that the bottomless pit gave way to today's lake: *"And you can still hear the crack of a whip, black gallops of horses, women yelling, the cry of babies and bells, deep in the dark waters, under a layer of centuries"*... A few years ago, it is said there was a glimpse of a placid crocodile known as "Birillo" in the lake waters. At sunset, try inspecting the waters of the lake, you never know!

The Tuscan Maremma is a land that evokes its rich past and, in particular, it is a place where the Etruscans and the Romans left their marks, full of discovery and magic. Fenice Capanne has a key location near the sea, which can be reached by car in twenty minutes. Follonica, thanks to its beautiful, well-equipped public beaches, is recognized as one of the most visited beaches in Tuscany. Located near Capanne, the Accesa Lake offers an alternative to the beach.

Food and Wine: a recipe not to be missed, as told by a Tuscan

I follow my "Ribollita" recipe just like my mother used to do - I eyeball it. First, you take some white kidney beans and let them soak overnight before cooking them in plenty of water. (You can also use canned organic beans. Two should be plenty, cook them for a bit with a sprig of rosemary and oil before mashing half of them and leaving the other half whole). Sauté some onion, leeks, carrot, and celery with olive oil (four or five tablespoons) in a saucepan. After a few minutes, add chopped Savoy cabbage, kale, chard, two potatoes cut in chunks, and four diced tomatoes before covering. In a separate pot, bring water and a vegetable-seasoning cube (without gluten) to a boil and add to the soup. Allow everything to boil for at least an hour and a half. Add some raw olive oil. At the halfway cooking point, add the mashed beans and whole beans. Add salt to taste, I also personally like to add a bit of red pepper flakes. Otherwise, I like to add some to each individual plate. This soup makes for perfect leftovers. Buon appetito!

How to get there

From Genova: take the A12-E80 highway in the direction of Livorno. Exit at Rosignano Marittimo (where the highway ends). Follow directions for Rome, on the Aurelia SS 1 bis (E80). Exit at Follonica Est-Massa Marittima. Follow directions for Massa Maritima.

From Florence: from the A1 highway, exit at Firenze-Certosa, then enter the state highway "Palio" Florence-Siena. Exit a Colle di Val d'Elsa Sud. Follow directions for Follonica-Grosseto, on the provincial road n. 541. After passing the enchanting Frosini castle, take the provincial road Massetana n. 441 for the city of Massa Marittima. After reaching the sign for "Città di Massa Marittima" (after the ESSO gas station), take an immediate right in the direction of Capanne. After 100 metres, turn left in the direction of Capanne.

From Rome: take the A12 highway toward Civitavecchia. Follow the road to the end of the highway, and enter onto the Via Aurelia E80, toward Follonica, exit Favorrano Scalo. Follow directions for Lago Accesa, and look for indications for Capanne.

Hotels and Bed and Breakfasts

La Locanda del Minatore – Loc. Fenice Capanne (Massa Marittima), tel. +39 0566-903742, fax 0566-903742.

Agriturismo Poggio Corbello – Via Poggio Corbello, 42, tel. +39 0566-919029.

PART FOUR

PUGLIA

As part of our ideal trip, and with the guidance of Garrone's film, Puglia could not be left out. The beauties of Puglia are often associated with the magnificent coastlines of the Ionian Sea to the south, and the Adriatic Sea to the east. However, beyond the crystal blue waters of Salento and Gargano, whose shores attract tourists from all over the world, anyone who visits this region of Italy is sure to find plenty of cultural attractions.

Throughout many places in Puglia, allurement and magic are often intertwined. It is therefore no mystery as to why Garrone chose to take the audience on a journey to the Castel del Monte.

Upon entering the castle that dominates the valley below, you almost expect to encounter the king flanked by the giant flea that would eventually cause much strife to the king's daughter and inspire one of the three tales told in Garrone's film. Puglia offered many riveting places for the scenography of the film. In fact, scenes from the ogre's house, who was set to marry the king's daughter, were filmed in the hypogeum village of the ravine of Petruscio, in Mottola. The castle was built in the 13th century, and was commissioned by emperor Frederick II in Puglia, in the territory of the Andria municipality about 18 km from the city in the area of Santa Maria del Monte, in the province of Barletta-Andria-Trani.

Positioned atop a hill of the Murge plateau, 540 metres above sea level, the castle was included in the list of national Italian monuments in 1936, and has been protected as a World Heritage landmark since 1996.

The large structure, whose original function is still unclear, is undoubtedly an architectural work of art, and the synthesis of refined mathematics, geometrics and astronomical knowledge. A few hypotheses suggest the castle was used as a wellness centre based on a model of an Arab *hamman*. Many elements of its construction seem to point to this theory; for example, the multiple and ingenious canal and water collection systems, the numerous conservation tanks, the presence of the oldest bathrooms in history, the unique structure of the complex as a whole, the one-way internal path and its octagonal layout.

Three types of material were used in the construction of the castle, which were deliberately chosen and artistically arranged in order to have a particular chromatic effect that intrigues the observer. Limestone is the primary material used and can be found in all of the architectural structures of the castle, and also in a few decorative elements. Thanks to this material, the colours of the castle fade from white to pink depending on the time of day. In a few of the rooms, white marble reminds visitors of its past use in the decorations of the building. The breccia corallina creates a refined effect that was supposed to be more pronounced seeing as each room was clad in this material. The octagon building is made up of two floors, which are connected by a counter-clockwise spiral staircase with forty-four trapezoidal steps.

The main entrance is on the east-facing wall, in other words in line with the position of the rising sun during the spring and autumn equinox. Two symmetrical staircases, reconstructed in 1928 and arranged in a pincer, are flanked alongside the entrance. The Castel del Monte became an official UNESCO landmark due to its mathematical and astronomical design, as well as for the harmony between cultural elements of northern Europe, the Islamic world and as a typical example of Medieval architecture.

The internal courtyard houses a large, functioning cistern used to collect rainwater along with five other similar cisterns. It could be said that the tall walls of the courtyard give the impression of being inside a water reservoir, which in the medieval period symbolized knowledge.

Puglia has much to offer lovers of discovery, so much so that it deserves at least one visit in a person's lifetime. If nothing else, just to say "I was there".

How to get there
Location: Comune of Andria (Bari), website: www.andrialive.it

By train: Arrive to Andria, and then continue by bus from Andria to Castel del Monte. Services run from the 1st of April to the 1st of November.

By car: Take the A14 highway (Bologna-Taranto), or the A16 highway (Bari-Napoli), and take the exit Andria-Barletta, SS 170 for about 18 km.

For more information:
www.ferrovienordbarese.it;
www.autolineeandriesi.it

As we follow in the footsteps of Garrone's film, our journey continues further south to Mottola. This small city, in the province of Taranto, sits atop one of the few "Tarantini" hills, about 387 metres above sea level. Its strategic geographical location inspired its nickname "Spia dello Ionio" or "The Ionian Spy" due to the fact that the Gulf of Taranto is visible from only a few points in the city. In the surrounding territory, the underground village of Petruscio is part of the ravine park. The rocky settlement was carved into one of the ravines, complete with "cave-houses" of multiple levels that were often connected by spectacular stairs carved into the rock. It goes without saying that this is one of the most beautiful places in the area. As was the case in other similar realities, these caves were used for human habitation, but were also used as shelters for animals, storage, work areas, stock rooms, churches and tombs making this the ideal location for Garrone's scenes of the ogre's dwelling where he takes the princess after correctly guessing the answer to the king's riddle.

Access to the village is limited to only a few roads, one of which is particularly difficult to navigate. The troglodyte village of Petruscio was carved and inhabited by the refugees of Mottola. The Saraceni destroyed it in 847, and it was abandoned until the end of the 12th century. Despite suffering numerous collapses over time, the medieval structures can still be seen today, as well as three churches (the "cathedral", the Polish church and the anonymous Glacis church), and the prison and refuge "De Rosa" whose namesake derives from the bandit who used it as a hiding place in the 19th century.

The "Casa dell'Igumeno", a small, two-story cave house, is an interesting aspect of the village. The ground floor is made up of the servants' quarters with the family residence on the main floor. Outside of the dwelling are washbasins for clothes, a bell-shaped cistern with small canals to collect rainwater, a drinking trough and a feeding trough for animals. The space reserved for daily interactions were separated from the animal shelters by a central structure. The store for hay is easily distinguishable, along with the area for equipment, a sewage trench, and fences for donkeys. Each space was rigorously carved into the rock.

Rainwater was conserved in the cisterns, however, whenever necessary, water was also taken from the river that ran along the bottom of the ravine. Looking down over the ravine to the river is an emotionally moving sight and allows the understanding of the natural means of defense by the inhabitants.

On the opposite side are about ten caverns covered in thriving vegetation and seemingly impenetrable. Further ahead are the ruins of the "Torre di Petruscio" that was once used for surveillance of the settlement. From there, a descending path leads to a steep set of steps in the shape of feet, and protected by a wooden handrail. In other words, it was a residence equipped with the most modern of comforts (for the time).

For more information and guided tours of the cliff dwellings, contact the Centro Comunale of Ricezione Turistica of the town of Mottola (Call: +39 009-8866928).

How to get there
From Mottola, follow the road (ex-statale 100) that goes to the train station and runs along the western side of the ravine. At the intersection with the street for Palagianello, a road sign to the left and a reception area indicate access to the village of Petruscio: Loc. Torre Petruscio, SS 100, 65 km.

For those who choose to visit the Capitanata, Ascoli Satriano is certainly one of the places that should not be left behind. Walking in the historic city centre and paying close attention to its numerous sites of historical-archaeological interest, you will discover that even the seemingly secondary and marginal areas conserve archaeological areas worthy of museums and international parks.

The prosperity of the town dates back the classical antiquity of the populace of this area, whose roots began in the 9th-8th century B.C., when an important Daunian cultural centre developed in the vast area that extends from the banks of the Carapelle to the hills occupied by the modern day town. Its prosperity also derives from its proliferate scientific activity, active for almost fifty years, that rendered the valley of the Carapelle one of the most preserved archaeological sites in Puglia. *Ausculum* is also famous for being the battleground between the Roman army and

Pyrrhus the king of Epirus in 279 B.C., and in 209 B.C. between the Romans and Hannibal's troops during the second Punic Wars. The centre came under Roman authority rather precociously, in part due to its close proximity to *Herdonia* and the Vie Appia and Traiana, and became a *municipium* in 89 B.C.

After visiting the cathedral, named after the nativity of the Virgin Mary and of Roman origin but intensely restored during the Renaissance and Baroque eras, the Palazzo Ducale, whose origin dates back to the 13th century, but seems to have been reconstructed several times with a dominating front entrance and crowned with a 'loggia' with arched windows, and after walking along the streets of the historic city centre, you will be ready to immerse yourself in the past by visiting the Museo Civico and Diocesano (open Tuesday-Sunday, 10am-12pm and 4pm-7pm: for guided tours, call +39 338-232-8894).

Housed in the Palazzo Vescovile, the museum preserves high quality collections dating back to funeral contexts of the Daunian era, and brought to light in the territory. Displayed are findings of very high intrinsic and symbolic value due to the chosen figurative and geometric decorations, the material used and the cultural influence depicted, as well as numerous imported products that take you on a journey through the discovery of funeral rituals of the Daunian elites from the 4th and 2nd century B.C.

That being said, the flagship of the museum is without question the marble artwork of a permanent installation titled "Policromie of the Sublime". The focal point of the installation is the *trapezoforos*, in other words the base of a funeral dining table in polychrome marble with two griffons biting a pricket. Along with the other impressive pieces of the exhibition, the griffin is a symbol of great pride for the Ascolan community, so much so that the city proclaimed itself as "The City of Griffins". Trade of the collection on the black market, its purchase by the Paul Getty Museum in Malibu and eventual transport to Rome, followed by a return to its point of origin are testament to the important and noteworthy findings. More recently, the *trapezoforos* was even included in the Italian pavilion at the Milan Expo in 2015.

The table dates back to the 4th century B.C. and is part of the furnishings of a room-like tomb of the Ascolano territory, and was stolen in the '70s. The adventurous past of the clandestine excavations, from its arrival in the Swiss *caveaux*, to trades with the famous Californian museum through art dealers, and the complex inquiries by the Carabinieri, is all retold in Fabio Isman's book titled "Predators of Lost Art: The Stealing of Archaeology in Italy" and is also narrated by the panels in the museum.

The Serpent's Hill

After a visit to the museum, you can take a break in one of the restaurants in the historical city centre, such as "Medievalis", "Il Canto del Gallo", or in some of the less centralized restaurants such as "Tenuta Rinaldi", "Agriturismo I Grifoni", or, a few metres from the site, the agritourism that gets its name and logo from another archaeological site to be discussed later, "La Faragola". After a break, you may continue to another archaeological site: the Serpent's Hill.

This hill overlooks the small city, and in the Daunian era it was a point of reference for the population and place of residence, as well as a tomb for noble families. Following inquiries by the University of Innsbruck and of Basilicata, and by the Supervision of Puglia, the Archaeological Park of Daunia was established here. The home of an upper-class family can still be visited (as suggested by external paving of river rocks, fragments of ceramics, evidence of a banquet hall, and the compartment used for food preservation). Large, rectangular sacred structures occupy the southeast section where processions and funeral rituals took place. An axis road made of river pebbles constitutes the processional road for funeral ceremonies of the high-class members of Daunian society. Human corpses were placed in small buildings known as *oikoi*, which faced the road. Inside these buildings, there was room for both the *prothesis*, or the exhibition of the body before burial, and the periodic banquets to commemorate the deceased. Do not forget to ask to visit the funerary situated directly outside the archaeological park.

The Roman Villa of Faragola

A tour must be scheduled ahead of time (for information and guided tours: ArcheoLogica services, call: +39 347-317-6098). Not to be missed is a visit to the "Piazza Armerina of Puglia", the Roman villa of Faragola. Discovered in 2003, and inspected over the course of ten long excavation campaigns by the University of Foggia, the villa became available by way of a museum tour accompanied by professional archaeologists. Many events and games for families are organized by the ArcheoLogica, as part of the SAC (Sistemi Ambiente Cultura) of the region of Puglia, within the archaeological environment where tours can be reserved. Built atop an old Daunian site, the villa dates back to the 6th century B.C. and is a perfect example of a countryside residence of an elite Roman family during the Imperial age and Late-Antiquity, who owned a large amount of land in *Apulia* and built their own luxurious mansion for themselves and their guests in the valley of the Carapelle. Inside the complex and expansive structure was the intersection of *fructus et luxuria*: production and luxury. As a matter of fact, the villa is comprised of a residential area, with a vast, outdoor dining room decorated in polychrome marble and panels in opus sectile, two thermal bath installations with impressive mosaics, bedrooms and courtyards and an ample production area where products from the fields were stored and where the *familia*, that is the slaves of the *dominus*, resided, dedicating their time to the working of clay, production of ceramics and handcrafts with bone and metals. During the Medieval period, the site underwent radical changes, but was lived in until the end of the 9th century. The wonders of this villa must be seen for yourself, and with your own eyes.

Cultural and Religious Events

A visit to Ascoli is a pleasure in springtime, during the warmer months of April and May, whereas a visit during the hot summer months when temperatures reach 43 degrees Celcius is not advisable and would most likely render tours to the archaeological sites quite unenjoyable.

The patron's celebration of the city occurs on the 14th of January when locals celebrate the protective saint of the city, Saint Potito Martire. The protagonist is the "ciuccio di cartone" or "cardboard donkey" stuffed with fireworks, in memory of the donkey that showed a wayfarer where to find the remains of Saint Potito.

If a single (but intense) day is enough to see the city centre, the archaeology museum, and the Faragola villa, then Ascoli would be a good point of departure to visit the surrounding areas (Bovino,

Herdonia, Canosa and Melfi). For those wishing to spend one or two nights, the various B&Bs in the city centre are good places to stay (B&B Ausculum, www.bbausculum.it; Alla corte del Duca, www. allacortedelduca.it). For those looking for a place outside of the city, "La Faragola" (www.lafaragola. it) is a good place to relax, and has two outdoor pools and a spa.

It is hard to understand what pushes tourists to climb the 600 metres to Orsara in Puglia. Perhaps it is the well-deserved culinary fame of the small city of Monti Dauini, or maybe it is the beauty of the historical city centre (TCI's orange flag), or the amazing view and surrounding landscapes. Perhaps it is for all of these reasons and then some. If you happen to visit during the first week of August, you can enjoy the famous Orsara Jazz Festival, one of the most renowned in Italy, right in the heart of the city. On the other hand, if you find yourself there in June, you can participate in the "Festa del Vino" (but be careful about driving afterwards because the quality and the alcohol percentage of these wines is very high, especially the Tuccanese, a typical Orsara wine that does not pair well with driving!). However, the most charming and fascinating tradition is the "Fucacoste" which takes place on the evening of November 1st, the longest night of the year, when the whole city is lit up with *falò* (*fucacoste*), or bonfires, *cocce priatorjie* (heads of purgatory) and jack-o-lanterns. This is an ancient custom that existed long before modern concepts of Halloween. The invoked spirits in Orsara have nothing to do with demons. In fact, the Christian interpretation of this pagan ritual was transformed into one that involves the souls of Purgatory, the deceased waiting to go to Heaven, thanks to the "purgation" symbolized by fire, as opposed to natural forces. The lights show the deceased the way to return to their place of origin while the pumpkins, with their carved mouths and eyes, grim and grotesque all at once, symbolize death and resemble the Purgatory souls waiting to get to paradise.

Before having a seat at the table, a visit in Orsara is not complete without learning about a few significant monuments: the Abbey of Angelo from the 12th century, Palazzo Baronale, originally a monastery, then the seat of Spanish knights of Calatrava and eventually passing to the family dynasty of the area, the Guevara, who turned the palace into an aristocratic residence. Another monumental site worth visiting is the cave of Saint Michael the Archangel, along the road of the pilgrimage toward the sanctuary of Monte Sant'Angelo on the Gargano River. The church of the Annunciation sits above the cave. A stroll can include the entire historic centre of the city, with noble palaces and the main church of Saint Nicholas of Bari.

Food and Wine

The main attraction of the city is the food, and thanks to its devotion to high quality cuisine it was awarded the honour of "Città del Buon Vivere", or the "City of Good Living" by the Slow Food organisation. Many restaurants offer the possibility of tasting traditional cuisine made with high quality products from the surrounding areas, such as vegetables, meat, cheeses, cured meats, and wine. The most famous chef is definitely Peppe Zullo who founded an international culinary school and had the prestige to create a true business that ensures high quality, healthy food by growing food in his own garden or cooking with local specialties such as wild boar (cinghiale), combining innovation and experimentation. In one of his restaurants, "Nuova Sala Paradiso", the "Cantina del Paradiso" is not to be missed, and contains a wonderful collection of wines housed in an exquisite architectural structure, defined by the biennial festival of Architecture in Venice as "one of the cathedrals of Italian wine".

The "forno a paglia", or straw oven bakery, of Angelo di Biccari's restaurant "Pane e Salute" or "Trilussa", founded in 1525, is sure to offer a unique experience. In this restaurant, customers can eat at a marble table near the fully functioning oven still capable of cooking huge loaves of homemade bread, as well as the delicious "scaldatelli" (crackers more commonly known as taralli), biscuits (cookies) and wonderful pizza. Of course, all of these treats are accompanied by a glass of Tuccanese, a ruby red wine with a touch of floral flavours made in a local winery dating back to the Middle Ages.

Sheltered by the Daunian hills, the small town center of Bovino faces the valley of the Cervaro River and is the perfect weekend destination in what could be considered the new Mediterranean triad of culture, nature and culinary arts.

The Touring Club of Italy awarded Bovino the Orange Flag as one of the most beautiful towns in Italy for its excellence and hospitality, and has something to offer all year long: in the summer you can enjoy fresh evenings sitting at 647 metres above sea level; the fields changing from brown to an intense yellow can be observed during the intermediate seasons; during the winter, paying close attention to the frequent snowfall that renders the hairpin turns rather impractical, the numerous restaurant environments (especially "La Cantina" owned by Nicola Consiglio) and the B&B and spa, "Le pietre del Borgo" (www.lepietredelborgo.it) offer a warm refuge from the cold. Some of the best times to visit Bovino are during the celebration of

San Celestino on the second Sunday of October, the culinary event "La disfida del Soffritto" in March-April, or during one of the many summer events organized by the city.

Accessing the city from the main entrance that goes from Corso Vittorio Emanuele to the centre of the ancient village, visitors not only step into the ancient history of the small city centre but also into the history of the entire territory that was once the capital of the region. Medieval Bovino was erected on the hill occupied during the Roman era by *Vibinum*, a colony founded during the Sillana era in a strategic location due to its position on the border between culturally and geographically diverse areas: the *Colonia Vibina* arose amidst *Apulia*, *Campania* and *Sannium* on the shores of the Adriatic Sea and the Tyrrhenian Sea, and between the mountains of the Subappennino and the plains of the Tavoliere.

There are various overlooks throughout the historic city centre that allow visitors to enjoy the spacious valley of the Cervaro River. As visitors look out over the river, they should try to imagine the role a river like this played in the organization of the settlement in the valley during ancient times. Neolithic villages, Bronze era settlements and numerous Roman era villas, the most famous of which is the villa of Casalene, populate the surrounding landscapes. The famous villa is comprised of a residential area and production area from the Augustus era and Late-Antiquity.

The characteristics of mixed cultures are even embedded inside the city walls. A visit to the Museo Civico (open Saturday and Sunday from 10:30am-12:30pm and 5:30pm-7:30pm; for special opening hours contact the ArcheoClub of Bovino) allows visitors to understand the evolution of the city centre and the surrounding territory between pre-history and the Middle Ages thanks to the archaeological exhibits. Of particular value are the anthropomorphic lithian stones dating back to the Eneolithic era, the Roman era ceramics, a sundial from the Roman villa of Casale, the numerous olive oil presses and the impressive private collection "Gennaro Marseglia" donated to the museum.

Several structures provide testimony of Roman dominance such as portions of the urban walls, mounted on the front of the medieval palaces near the so-called "Buco di San Marco", near the Lastene area and in the walls of the castle, the numerous underground environments (a cistern for conserving water, filled by the Roman aqueducts to supply water to the *domus* and the public baths), as well as pillars of the aqueduct in *opus quasi reticolatum*, visible in the area of a modern farm 3 km southeast of Bovino on the street that leads to Deliceto.

Although much pleasure comes from losing yourself among the small, well-maintained streets, the cathedral, the castle, and the small church of Saint Peter cannot go unseen.

The cathedral, named after Santa Maria Assunta was built in the 12th century on top of a pre-existing Early Christian church, whereas its façade displaying the early influences of the Gothic style of architecture, was rebuilt in 1231 and is a perfect example of reusing materials. Visitors can have fun recognizing pieces of Roman architecture reused in the medieval church.

The castle, on the other hand, occupies the western spur of Bovino and was built by Drogone, the count of Puglia in the Norman era. The only remaining structure of the castle is the circular tower on the barbacane pyramidal trellis that imitates the pyramid of Caio Cestio in Rome. The fortress was enlarged by Frederick II and then reshaped in 1536 by the noble Guevara family who controlled the domain of Bovino for three centuries and built a luxurious residence with a library, an art gallery and expensive furniture. Walking through the dominating driveway, you can access the internal courtyard that faces the Museo Diocesano (open every day by reservation), the Clock Tower and a refine B&B "Residenza Ducale". The stairs lead to a breath-taking view of the city and the plains of Tavoliere. Bovino lights up at sunset like a modern day nativity scene, and on clear days you can see all the way to the Gulf of Manfredonia and Gargano.

How to get there

Getting to Bovino is particularly enjoyable for passionate cyclists. The most simple and accessible looped road begins from Foggia on the SS 90 toward Bovino Scalo where visitors can see the ancient post office and "Lo Mulino", an ancient water mill still in use today for grinding wheat, as well as take a moment to refresh in the family-owned restaurant "Fernando". More venturesome cyclists can then ascend toward the historic city centre, or continue along the SS 110 toward Castelluccio dei Sauri, deviating toward Ponte Rotto on the SP 108 to return to Foggia (about three and a half hours), having crossed animated landscapes like the plains of Tavoliere on the left, and the Daunian Hills to the right near the ancient Cerbalus.

PART FIVE

SICILY

As we reach the end our fantastic journey following in the footsteps of the plot of the film "Tale of Tales", it would not be complete without a quick jump over to Sicily. The region attracts many tourists with its natural, cultural and artistic beauties, and therefore comes as no surprise that Garrone pinpointed the castle of Donnafugata and the Alcantara Gorge as the setting for the tale of "The Queen".

The Castle of Donnafugata

Amongst the various hypotheses about the name "Donnafugata", it is necessary to consider the legend of Queen Blanche of Navarre, widow of King Martin I of Aragon, who was imprisoned in the castle by Count Bernardo Cabrera so he could marry her and become king. Information and documentation surrounding the legend are scarce, but the most accredited seems to be connected to the Chiaramonte family, counts of Modica in the 14th century. Vincenzo Arezzo-La

Rocca later purchased the estate of Donnafugata in 1648, and turned it in to his country home.

The castle of Donnafugata is in the contrada of Donnafugata about 15 km from Ragusa. The name attributed to the castle may suggest that it is more of a lavish noble villa of the late 1800s rather than an actual castle.

Family descendants were responsible for enlarging the estate, and after various generations it was passed to Clementina Paternò of Manganelli, the widow of viscount Gaetano Combre de Lestrade. However, over the years, people lost interest in the castle and it was neglected to the point of complete abandonment. In 1928 it was purchased and restored by the municipality of Ragusa, making it available to the public.

The prestigious estate of more than 120 rooms is three stories high and overlooks a garden and the enchanting countryside. About twenty rooms can be visited, each one admirable for its original furniture and luxurious décor.

The castle is surrounded by a large, 8 hectare park with about 1500 species of plants and a few artefacts such as the small, round temple, the "Coffee House", and the unique stone labyrinth constructed in typical Ragusan masonry where Garrone filmed a beautiful scene with the Mexican actress in a red brocade gown as she painfully chases her son Elias.

It may be surprising that the Ragusa-Comiso train station sits just a few hundred metres from the castle, almost as if the baron Corrado Arezzo de Spuches of Donnafugata used his political influence to have it there, and is no doubt rather convenient for tourists.

Besides Garrone's film, the castle has provided the set for several movie and television scenes over the years. Scenes from the film "I Vicerè" were filmed in the "billiard hall", whereas scenes from the TV series "Il commissario Montalbano" were filmed on the balcony.

The Alcantara Gorge

In the valley of Alcantara, where the Peloretani mountain chain ends between the cities of Castiglione of Sicily and Motta Camastra, a unique panorama reveals itself to visitors. The Alcantara Gorge is part of the Alcantara Park, established in 2001 in place of the pre-existing reserve. It includes part of the territories of the province of Messina and Catania that form the river basin of the Alcantara River and is situated on the north side of Mount Etna.

The fascinating and mysterious gorge is unforgettable, and while it seems as though it was formed by water erosion over thousands of years, reality tells a different story. It is presumed that ancient earthquakes split the volcanic rock and created space for the riverbed.

This riverbed has existed since prehistoric and protohistoric eras, and many lava flows before the time of Mount Etna have obstructed and modified its path. The water route is known for its nearly 50-meter high walls about 4-5 metres wide. Looking up river is like looking into the womb of the Earth. This mystical feeling is enhanced by the small amount of sunshine that reflects on the crystal clear water droplets hanging on the black walls.

The scenery is truly unique and surreal. Scenes from Garrone's film seem so magical and timeless that it makes you wonder at the reconstruction of the scenography. The king of Selvascusa goes in search of the dragon with the intention of ripping out its heart on behalf of his beloved queen's desire for a child. The heart is to be cooked by a virgin and eaten by the wife. Dressed in armour, the king plunges himself into the freezing waters of the Alcantara gorge to find the monster. The moment the king immerses himself into the water, the typical shapes of "cataste di legna" (firewood) and "colonne d'organo" (organ columns) of the walls can easily be seen.

The main office of the park is in Francavilla di Sicilia, in a building that was originally built as a day care for children but was never used, whereas the Centre for Research, Training, and Environmental Education is in the municipality of Castiglione di Sicilia. The Ente Parco Fluviale of Alcantara, a public entity under the control and supervision of the Sicilian region, manages the park.

The route for visiting the canyon starts from the initial path of the valley amongst small lakes and waterfalls of pure water. There is a small beach at the entrance to the gorge and is accessible during the summer months until the water levels begin exceeding safety limits, in which case visitors can take the "Sentiero delle Gole" (The Gorge Path) up the left river bank. This path crosses over cultivated fields for about 1 km and allows you to reach breath-taking panoramic views such as "La Terrazza di Venere" (The Balcony of Venus) or "Il Balcone delle Muse" (The Balcony of the Muses). Otherwise, river trekking and body rafting are the two most adventurous options for experiencing the gorge.

The Alcantra River Park includes the towns it crosses through. The closest one to the coast is Giardini Naxos (Naxos Gardens), followed by Taormina, Calatabiano, famous for its medieval castle, Gaggi, Graniti, known for its cherry production, and Motta Camastra, the starting point for exploring the gorge and other small towns.

How to get there

To get to the Alcantara Gorge, you must pass by the Naxos Gardens in the direction of Francavilla di Sicilia for about 12 km.

<u>From Messina</u>: take the A18 highway in the direction of Catania and exit at Giardini Naxos.

<u>From Catania</u>: take the A18 highway in the direction of Messina and exit at Giardini Naxos.

We have officially reached the end of our quest through the wonders of this "beautiful country", visited by millions of people every year. This books hopes to be the stimulus for an unusual route that leads to the discovery of the most beautiful, yet less noted, parts of the Italian territory, while respecting the rules of safeguarding and conservation.

Naturally, many thanks must be given to Matteo Garrone who opened many people's eyes, even the most distracted of people, by offering a reason to reflect on the beauties at our fingertips, and give direction to thoughts of our next adventure.

We have completed our journey, full of forests, monuments and cities. We saw, savoured, touched and smelled. One who does not travel does not discover and rediscover the corners of their mind. We have an ability to remember and recall our deepest, and most preserved memories, but none of us would have a future without a present. Bringing a dormant thought to life by seeing a mountain stream, detecting an ancient scent and listening to the sound of cracking sticks under our feet, can revive feelings and emotions we believed to be lost long ago just because we forgot to have ever lived them.

Perhaps those who never travel or read never truly live, for reading takes you on a journey of enjoyment through the beauty of the world without ever leaving your seat, and living life to the fullest by remaining still and seeing the world through eyes of imagination and disenchantment.

Those who stop dreaming, who no longer allow their mind to fly far, far away where the river runs, where the wind caresses the tree branches and rustles the leaves, where clouds become thunderstorms, where thunderstorms become hurricanes and sweeps away the motionless reader, will truly perish.

Those who do not take time to enjoy a monument, or a statue with its realistic appearance in the way it presents its nudity, or an enchanting landscape where the houses seem to lean against the soft slope of the hill, those who do not experience its greatness will truly perish.

Those who do not read, who do not wish to see beyond the end of their own nose for fear that something might reveal real people living in enchanted worlds, will truly perish.

Acknowledgements

I would like to thank those who contributed to the stories of the places described in this book: Ombretta Sarchioni: Torre Alfina; Cooperativa "L'Ape Regina": Acquapendente; Gianluca Forti: The Flower Museum of Acquapendente; Maria Grazia Fontana: Viterbo, Villa Lante di Bagnaia; Paola Di Scanno: Arpino; Lara Lorenzetti: Fenice Capanne; Valeria Volpe: Orsara, Ascoli Satriano, Bovino; Massimo Sottani: The Castle of Sammezzano.

I would also like to give special thanks to Giovanmatteo Raggi for believing in this book.

Photographs
Valeria Volpe, Claudio Venturelli, Caterina Maseddu, Maria Grazia Fontana, Paola Di Scanno, Alessandro Frignani, Gaia Venturelli, Domenico Giangiordano.

Recipes

The "ribollita" toscana by Elisabetta Boninsegna; "sagne e fagioli" by Paola Di Sanno; "crostone, cavolo nero e fagioli zolfini" by Massimo Sottani.

APPENDIX OF PHOTOGRAPHS

Index

NOTES

Fondazione
Apulia felix

The book supports the *Fondazione Apulia felix Onlus* in order to enhance its social, cultural, and territorial studies.

The *Fondazione Apulia felix Onlus* initiative was founded in 2012 by a few entrepreneurial groups of Foggia who wanted to give a clear signal to the local community by personally working hard, not only with resources but above all with true experience and a desire to help. In just a few years, professionals and citizens, such as business partners and volunteer participants, have joined the cause in support of the construction of a service organization for the city of Foggia and the territories of Capitanata and Puglia, and above all for its citizens in the cultural, social, and informative realms.

Historica Publishing
historicaedizioni.com
info@historicaweb.com